JOURNEY
with
DAVID BRAINERD

Forty days
or forty nights
with
David Brainerd

InterVarsity Press
Downers Grove

D0770472

InterVarsity Press is the
book publishing division
of Inter-Varsity Christian
Fellowship, a student movement
active on campus at hundreds
of universities, colleges and
schools of nursing. For information
about Inter-Varsity Christian
Fellowship, write IVCF,
233 Langdon, Madison WI 53703.

ISBN 0-87784-640-5
Library of Congress Catalog
Card Number: 74-20100

Printed in the United
States of America

To Arlene, my wife

CONTENTS

Introduction

"A Great Awakening or a Gentle Stir?" is the question raised by recent interpreters of the Jesus people.[1] Such a question might well be applied to the general religious excitement of the 1970s. It is probably too early to render a sound verdict about the religious enthusiasm of our present decade, but no one can dispute the fact that an extraordinary number of people are searching passionately for a direct, immediate and personal experience of God.

To assist such people, especially those who are seeking a dynamic spiritual experience within the evangelical Christian tradition, I have gathered together in a devotional guide selected excerpts from the diary, journal and letters of David Brainerd. Brainerd (1718-47) is chiefly known as the young, courageous missionary to the Indians during the Great Awakening of our early colonial history. Jonathan Edwards was the first to recognize that Brainerd was also a master of the devotional life and that his singular example of personal dedication was "most worthy of imitation."[2]

To be sure, we cannot or should not attempt to duplicate his exact journey, but if we spend time traveling vicariously with him we are certain to capture something of his intense desire to know and serve God and of his creative blending of the contemplative and active aspects of religious faith into one surrendered life.

What specifically can Brainerd offer us as we pursue our own quest for a more profound encounter with God?

First, Brainerd provides us with *an extraordinary example of absolute devotion to God.* In an age when many people in government, in business, in labor, in the home and even in the church are compromising or negating their personal commitments, it is refreshing to meet a completely dedicated person. Few people have ever thirsted after God as did this man. He gives us a unique model of religious intensity.

Second, Brainerd assists us in *distinguishing between superficial piety and authentic Christian experience.* He is always careful to differentiate between what he calls *true religion* and *false religion.* His perceptions challenge all sham, exhibitionism, emotionalism and dissention in America's present religious awakening. Today we need his kind of prayerful introspection that centers not so much upon subjective feelings but rather upon the glory of God.

Third, Brainerd inspires us *to engage in missionary service.* The devotional discipline is not an end in itself; on the contrary, it is preparation for the life of service. His memoirs edited and published by Edwards became a motivating force in the Great Awakening as well as in later evangelical revivals in Great Britain and America as attested by the writings of John Wesley and Francis Asbury. Furthermore, the memoirs furnished impetus to the modern missionary movement, influencing directly such pioneer missionaries to India as William Carey and Henry Martyn. In our own generation, Jim Elliot, who labored among the Auca Indians of South America, had as his constant companion these same memoirs which he consulted faithfully. Brainerd's missionary ardor is contagious.

Fourth, Brainerd instills in us *a compassionate empathy for the forgotten and dispossessed peoples of the world.* At the beginning of his mission to the Indians he endured a painful period of acculturation, but in time he came to identify completely with them and to love them, in his words, as "my dear flock." He was one of the few white persons of his day who really understood the Indians and who sought to live and work constructively with them. In our own time, when we are gaining a fresh appreciation of our American Indian heritage and seeking ways and means to insure dignity, well-being and promise to these our brothers, Brainerd's experience has special pertinence.

My primary source has been Sereno E. Dwight's edition of the *Memoirs of the Rev. David Brainerd; Missionary to the Indians . . . Chiefly Taken from His Own Diary by Rev. Jonathan Edwards . . .* printed and published by S. Converse at New Haven in 1822. Dwight's edition is especially valuable because it is the first edition to include a complete collection of Brainerd's writings in chronological order. The *Memoirs* encompass not only Brainerd's private *Diary* but also his *Journal* (Reports to the Commissioners of the Society in Scotland for Propagating Christian Knowledge) and important personal letters. I have selected a variety of excerpts from his writings and arranged them in a series of forty meditations consisting of a major theme, the text itself and a prayer of my own to aid the reader in interacting with Brainerd's thoughts. The selections are not meant to be read merely as history or biography. Rather, they are to be read creatively in the same devotional spirit in which they were first written. I have divided the selections into a fivefold pattern: personal commitment, pilgrimage for God's glory, the dark night of the soul, the great awakening and union with God. In certain respects such a division parallels key stages in the traditional mystical way, but in some instances Brainerd's approach differs, as we shall see later.

The reader is invited to begin a journey with David Brainerd. The journey is to be traveled on two levels: One is internal, the way of mysticism; the other is external, the way of mission. But it is one journey supremely dedicated to the glory of God. This devotional manual is based upon the firm conviction that Brainerd is an excellent mentor to guide not only theological students, ministers and missionaries but all Christians who seek a deeper devotional life and a more effective personal witness. Perhaps a fresh reading of these selections from Brainerd's *Memoirs* will once again motivate a few young men and women to serve on one of the difficult mission fields at home or in a distant land among the lonely, forgotten and disenchanted people of the world.

PERSONAL COMMITMENT

Haddam, Connecticut,
where David Brainerd was born.

"Extraordinarily sensitive, a mystic, deeply devoted, although David Brainerd died young he exercised a profound influence. His diary was widely read and helped to inspire many to become missionaries, not only in America, but also in other parts of the world."[1]

Kenneth Scott Latourette,
eminent historian of Christian missions

The journey of the spirit is a long process, but it begins somewhere. The point of origin is obscure for some travelers. Dag Hammarskjold wrote, "I don't know Who—or what—put the question, I don't know when it was put. I don't even remember answering. But at some moment I did answer Yes to Someone —or something."[2] The date of personal commitment is precise for other adventurers of the spirit. Senator Mark Hatfield (like Hammarskjold, a man who combines the contemplative and active lives) was definite about his transforming moment. He writes, "I made the choice that night [in 1954], many years ago; I *committed* myself to Christ. I saw that for thirty-one years I had lived for self, and I decided I wanted to live the rest of my life for Jesus Christ."³ David Brainerd was more like Hatfield than Hammarskjold in that he too could point to a clear-cut time on a summer evening in his twenty-first year when he entered what he described as a "new world."

Born in Haddam, Connecticut, on April 20, 1718, the sixth of nine children, he was reared in a strict Puritan home and was made conscious at an early age of his religious "duties" of prayer, Bible reading and worship. It was not until 1739 as a young man that he experienced conversion. In September of that same year he entered Yale College at New Haven where he proved to be an able student and leader of his class. His college years were interrupted by sieges of illness which forced him to return to Haddam for recuperation. He was already beginning to exhibit the first signs of the terrifying disease of tuberculosis that was to afflict him throughout his ministry and lead to his premature death at the age of twenty-nine.

When the Great Awakening burst forth among the students at the college, Brainerd became one of the revival's most enthusiastic supporters and was impatient with anyone who did not share his excitement. One day he made a statement about Mr. Chauncey Whittelsey, one of his professors, saying, "He has no more grace than this chair."⁴ When the president of the college learned of Brainerd's remarks, he displayed little appreciation for such criticism and had him expelled in 1742. Later, a more mature Brainerd was to regret his rash charge. He tried repeatedly to be reinstated and receive his degree but all his pleas were unsuccessful. Throughout the remainder of his life he was very sensitive about criticism and division and became a strong advocate of unity and harmony among Christians.

After leaving Yale, Brainerd prepared for the ministry by studying with Jedediah Mills, pastor at Ripton, ten miles from New Haven. During this period of apprenticeship he dedicated himself fully to God's service and began to contemplate the prospects of a mission to the Indians.

The following selections describe Brainerd's initial striving to please God, his "new inward apprehension of God" that transformed his life, his struggle to reconcile his conversion experience with his intellectual studies at Yale, his unconditional surrender to God's service and finally his resolve to live for God and nothing but God himself. Before we can probe the deeper levels of Christian devotion, we too must begin with a similar personal commitment.

The Journey Begins

"I read the calls of Christ to the weary and heavy laden; but could find no way that he directed them to come in. I thought I would gladly come, if I knew how; though the path of duty were never so difficult." (p. 42)

"After a considerable time spent in similar exercises and distresses, one morning, while I was walking in a solitary place, as usual, I at once saw that all my contrivances and projects to effect or procure deliverance and salvation for myself, were utterly in vain; I was brought quite to a stand, as finding myself totally lost. I had thought many times before, that the difficulties in my way were very great; but now I saw, in another and very different light, that it was for ever impossible for me to do anything towards helping or delivering myself. I then thought of blaming myself, that I had not done more and been more engaged, while I had opportunity—for it seemed now as if the season of doing was for ever over and gone. . . .

"While I remained in this state, my notions respecting my duties were quite different from what I had ever entertained in times past. . . . now, the more I did in prayer or any other duty, the more I saw that I was indebted to God for allowing me to ask for mercy; for I saw that self-interest had led me to pray, and that I had never once prayed from any respect to the glory of God. . . . I saw that I had been heaping up my devotions before God, fasting, praying, &c. pretending, and indeed really thinking sometimes, that I was aiming at the glory of God; whereas I never once truly intended it, but only my own happiness. . . . I saw that something worse had attended my duties than barely a few wanderings; for the whole was nothing but self-worship, and an horrid abuse of God." (pp. 45-46)

Prayer

O Lord, my spiritual journey begins with a determined effort to know you by my own strivings and to impress you by my own good works. And yet I soon learn that the path of self-interest leads to a dead end and that I neither discover you nor my own true self. Grant that my ultimate trust will be not in my own strivings and good works but in your grace alone disclosed in Jesus Christ my Lord. Amen.

A New Inward Apprehension

2 "I continued, as I remember, in this state of mind, from Friday morning till the Sabbath evening following (July 12, 1739) when I was walking again in the same solitary place, where I was brought to see myself lost and helpless, as before mentioned. Here, in a mournful melancholy state, I was attempting to pray; but found no heart to engage in that or any other duty; my former concern, exercise, and religious affections were now gone. I thought that the Spirit of God had quite left me; . . . then, as I was walking in a dark thick grove, unspeakable glory seemed to open to the view and apprehension of my soul. I do not mean any external brightness, for I saw no such thing; nor do I intend any imagination of a body of light, some where in the third heavens, or any thing of that nature; but it was a new inward apprehension or view that I had of God, such as I never had before, nor any thing which had the least resemblance of it. I stood still; wondered; and admired! I knew that I never had seen before any thing comparable to it for excellency and beauty; it was widely different from all the conceptions that ever I had of God, or things divine. I had no particular apprehension of any one person in the Trinity, either the Father, the Son, or the Holy Ghost; but it appeared to be Divine glory. My soul rejoiced with joy unspeakable, to see such a God, such a glorious divine Being; and I was inwardly pleased and satisfied that he should be God over all for ever and ever. My soul was so captivated and delighted with the excellency, loveliness, greatness, and other perfections of God, that I was even swallowed up in him; at least to that degree, that I had no thought (as I remember) at first, about my own salvation, and scarcely reflected that there was such a creature as myself.

"Thus God, I trust, brought me to a hearty disposition to exalt him, and set him on the throne, and principally and ultimately to aim at his honour and glory, as King of the universe. I continued in this state of inward joy, peace, and astonishment till near dark, without any sensible abatement; and then began to think and examine what I had seen; and felt sweetly composed in my mind all the evening following. I felt myself in a new world. . . . At this time, the way of salvation opened to me with such infinite wisdom, suitableness and excellency, that I wondered I should ever think of any other way of salvation; was amazed that I had not dropped my own contrivances, and complied with this lovely, blessed, and excellent way before. If I could have been saved by my own duties, or any other way that I had formerly contrived, my whole soul would now have refused it. I wondered that all the world did not see and comply with this way of salvation, entirely by the righteousness of Christ." (pp. 46-47)

Prayer

For the creative, transforming moments of life, I praise you, O God. Move me beyond all self-interest to a "new inward apprehension" of your presence so that I may perceive you as you really are. I was made to live in this "new world" where I can be lost in wonder and praise at your infinite beauty, excellence and love. Hear my prayer in the name of Christ my Savior and Lord. Amen.

Piety and Knowledge

3 "In the beginning of September [1739] I went to Yale College, and entered there; but with some degree of reluctancy, fearing lest I should not be able to lead a life of strict religion, in the midst of so many temptations." (p. 48)

"Some time in August following, I became so weakly and disordered, by too close application to my studies, that I was advised by my tutor to go home, and disengage my mind from study as much as I could; for I was grown so weak, that I began to spit blood. I took his advice, and endeavoured to lay aside my studies. But being brought very low, I looked death in the face more steadfastly; and the Lord was pleased to give me renewedly a sweet sense and relish of divine things; and particularly October 13, I found divine help and consolation in the precious duties of secret prayer and self-examination, and my soul took delight in the blessed God." (p. 49)

"I returned to college about Nov. 6, and, through the goodness of God, felt the power of religion almost daily, for the space of six weeks. . . . I longed to be conformed to God in all things. A day or two after, I enjoyed much of the light of God's countenance, most of the day; and my soul rested in God." (p. 50)

"I was in a comfortable frame of soul most of the day; but especially in evening devotions, when God was pleased wonderfully to assist and strengthen me; so that I thought nothing should ever move me from the love of God in Christ Jesus my Lord. Oh! one hour with God infinitely exceeds all the pleasures and delights of this lower world." (p. 50)

"Towards the latter end of January 1741, I grew more cold and dull in religion, by means of my old temptation, viz. ambition in my studies. But through divine goodness, a great and general Awakening spread itself over the college, about the latter end of February, in which I was much quickened, and more abundantly engaged in religion." (pp. 50-51)

Prayer

How do I balance the warm piety of my new life with the rational inquiry of my intellectual studies, O Lord? I sense that both emphases are necessary to prepare myself to serve you. Enable me, therefore, to develop a creative tension between the two so that heart and mind may be integrated in singleness of purpose in the doing of your will, in Jesus' name. Amen.

Unconditional Surrender

4 "I set apart this day for fasting and prayer to God for his grace; especially to prepare me for the work of the ministry; to give me divine aid and direction, in my preparations for that great work, and in his own time to send me into his harvest. Accordingly, in the morning, I endeavoured to plead for the divine presence for the day, and not without some life. In the forenoon, I felt the power of intercession for precious, immortal souls; for the advancement of the kingdom of my dear Lord and Saviour in the world; and withal, a most sweet resignation, and even consolation and joy, in the thoughts of suffering hardships, distresses, and even death itself, in the promotion of it; and had peculiar enlargement in pleading for the enlightening and conversion of the poor Heathen. In the afternoon, God was with me of a truth. O, it was blessed company indeed! God enabled me so to agonize in prayer, that I was quite wet with perspiration, though in the shade, and the cool wind. My soul was drawn out very much from the world, for multitudes of souls. . . . Oh that I may always live to and upon my blessed God! Amen, Amen.

"This day [April 20, 1742] I am twenty-four years of age. O how much mercy have I received the year past! How often has God caused his goodness to pass before me! And how poorly have I answered the vows I made . . . to be wholly the Lord's, to be forever devoted to his service! The Lord help me to live more to his glory for the time to come. This has been a sweet, a happy day for me; blessed be God. I think my soul was never drawn out in intercession for others, as it has been this night. Had a most fervent wrestle with the Lord to-night for my enemies; and I hardly ever so longed to live to God, and to be altogether devoted to him, I wanted to wear out my life in his service, and for his glory." (pp. 58-59)

Prayer

Almighty and everlasting God I yearn to reach such a stage in my own travels whereby I too can cry: "Lord, I want to wear out my life in your service and for your glory." May such a total commitment become the driving force of my life in the name and for the sake of Jesus. Amen.

Nothing But God Himself

5 "I retired pretty early for secret devotions; and in prayer, God was pleased to pour such ineffable comforts into my soul, that I could do nothing for some time but say over and over, O my sweet Saviour! 'O my sweet Saviour! whom have I in Heaven but thee? and there is none upon earth that I desire beside thee.' If I had had a thousand lives, my soul would gladly have laid them all down at once, to have been with Christ. My soul never enjoyed so much of heaven before; it was the most refined and most spiritual season of communion with God, I ever yet felt. I never felt so great a degree of resignation in my life." (p. 60)

"I withdrew to my usual place of retirement, in great peace and tranquility; spent about two hours in secret duties, and felt much as I did yesterday morning, only weaker, and more overcome. I seemed to depend wholly on my dear Lord; wholly weaned from all other dependences. I knew not what to say to my God, but only lean on his bosom, as it were, and breathe out my desires after a perfect conformity to him in all things. Thirsting desires and insatiable longings, possessed my soul after perfect holiness. God was so precious to my soul, that the world, with all its enjoyments, was infinitely vile. I had no more value for the favour of men, than for pebbles. The Lord was my ALL, and that he over-ruled all, greatly delighted me. . . . O that God would purge away my dross, and take away my tin, and make me ten times refined!" (p. 61)

"Had the most ardent longings after God, which I ever felt in my life. At noon, in my secret retirement, I could do nothing but tell my dear Lord, in a sweet calm, that he knew I desired nothing but himself, nothing but holiness; that he had given me these desires, and he only could give the thing desired. I never seemed to be so unhinged from myself, and to be so wholly devoted to God. My heart was swallowed up in God most of the day." (p. 65)

Prayer

Search my inner thoughts, O God. Test my motivation. Am I living for my own self or for your will? Do I really seek you above everything else? Is my prayer, like Brainerd's, to desire nothing but yourself? Grant that I may delight in you and you alone. Amen.

II
PILGRIMAGE FOR GOD'S GLORY

Kaunaumeek, now Brainerd, New York,
where Brainerd began his mission.

"Read David Brainerd today and yesterday, and find as usual my spirit greatly benefited by it. I long to be like him; let me forget the world and be swallowed up in a desire to glorify God."[1]

Henry Martyn,
English pioneer missionary to India

All who follow the mystic way begin with an initial resolve or personal commitment similar to that of Brainerd. From that point the pioneers of the devotional life proceed systematically to sharpen their awareness of God. "Purgation, illumination, union," writes Georgia Harkness, "—this is the threefold journey of the *scala perfectionis* which culminates in the vision of eternity within time."[2] I have used the phrase *pilgrimage for God's glory* to describe Brainerd's concept of the first stage, purgation. According to him, it was a time of rigorous self-discipline involving fasting, Bible reading, meditation and above all constant prayer. The purging process was absolutely essential if he was to live not for self but for God's glory.

In following Brainerd's exploration of the inner life, we may not fully appreciate in every respect his theological jargon and his devotional style. But as Robert Paul reminds us, "Despite the barbarities of our theologies and the morbid preoccupations of our inadequate devotions, to become a disciple of Jesus Christ and to meditate upon his passion is to catch something of the vision which sees 'the light of the knowledge of the glory of God in the face of Jesus Christ' (2 Cor. 4:6)."[3]

The external history of Brainerd's journey which parallels the selections from his *Memoirs* included in part II covers the period between the summer of 1742 and the summer of 1745. After having been licensed to preach by the Congregational Association meeting in Danbury on July 29, 1742, Brainerd received his first assignment, which was to engage in missions work among the Indians at Kaunaumeek—situated about halfway between Stockbridge, Massachusetts, and Albany, New York. Though he painstakingly learned the Indian language, his success at Kaunaumeek was rather limited. After a year's work he encouraged the few Indians in the area to relate themselves to John Sargent's already established mission station at Stockbridge and decided to move to a more promising mission field.

From the outset Brainerd's mission work had been sponsored by the Society in Scotland for the Propagation of Christian Knowledge and was supervised by "commissioners" who represented the Society's interests in the mission among the American Indians. The commissioners included some of the most prominent ministers in the New York area, including Ebenezer Pemberton of New York, Aaron Burr of Newark and Jonathan Dickinson of Elizabethtown. The middle section of Brainerd's *Memoirs* consists of a journal or progress report to the Society.

From this point on Brainerd's ecclesiastical relationship was with the Presbyterian church. Later entries in his diary record the fact that on numerous occasions he interrupted his missionary labors to attend faithfully the meetings of Presbytery. It was a relatively easy transition to make from New England Congregationalism to the prorevivalistic Presbyterianism of the Middle Colonies. In fact, there was a remarkable unity among all the evangelicals who favored the Great Awakening, a unity which embraced not only Congregationalists and Presbyterians but also Anglicans, Methodists, Baptists, Reformed and other Christians.

Ordained by the Presbytery of New York in Newark on June 12, 1744, Brainerd was commissioned to a new work among the Delaware Indians. His headquarters now became the Forks of the Delaware, near present-day Easton, Pennsylvania. In this region of the Delaware he labored once again with little visible success. While serving in this area, he made four excursions to the Susquehanna River where he lived and ministered to the Indians in such places as Juniata and Shamokin, near present-day Sunbury, Pennsylvania.

His diary during this period contains graphic pictures of his travels over the beautiful but rugged terrain of Eastern Pennsylvania and also intimate glimpses of Indian communal life, including their religious rituals and the practice of witchcraft. Despite the difficulties of his travels and the discouragement of the meager response of the Indians to his Christian message, Brainerd persisted in his inner pilgrimage to rid himself of all selfish motives and to live wholly to the honor and glory of God—whether or not he could report to the commissioners that he prospered in his mission.

The following selections give us further insight into Brainerd's intense devotional life. The first excerpt is part of a letter that he wrote to his brother, Israel, in which he outlined a few basic guidelines for one about to begin a spiritual journey. The main body of the selections consists of representative samples of his prayers arranged according to the classic division of adoration, confession, thanksgiving, petition and intercession. Brainerd is an astute guide for the person who wishes to learn to pray more effectively.

Guidelines for the Journey

6 "There is but one thing that deserves our highest care and most ardent desires; and that is, that we may answer the great end for which we were made, viz. to glorify that God, who has given us our being and all our comforts, and do all the good we possibly can to our fellow-men, while we live in the world. Verily life is not worth the having, if it be not improved for this noble end and purpose. Yet, alas, how little is this thought of among mankind! Most men seem to live to themselves without much regard to the glory of God, or the good of their fellow creatures. They earnestly desire, and eagerly pursue after the riches, the honours, and the pleasures of life, as if they really supposed, that wealth or greatness, or merriment could make their immortal souls happy. But alas! what false and delusive dreams are these! . . .

"If you would glorify God, or answer his just expectations from you, and make your own soul happy in this and the coming world, observe these few directions. . . .

"First, Resolve upon and daily endeavour to practise a life of seriousness and strict sobriety. The wise man will tell you the great advantage of such a life, Ecc. vii. 3. Think of the life of Christ; and when you can find that he was pleased with jesting and vain merriment, then you may indulge in it yourself.

"Again; Be careful to make a good improvement of precious time. When you cease from labour, fill up your time in reading, meditation, and prayer; and while your hands are labouring, let your heart be employed, as much as possible, in divine thoughts.

"Further; Take heed that you faithfully perform the business which you have to do in the world, from a regard to the commands of God; and not from an ambitious desire of being esteemed better than others. We should always look upon ourselves as God's servants, placed in God's world, to do his work; and accordingly labour faithfully for him; not with a design to grow rich and great, but to glorify God, and to do all the good we possibly can.

"Again: Never expect any satisfaction or happiness from the world. If you hope for happiness in the world, hope for it from God, and not from the world. Do not think you shall be more happy if you live to such or such a state of life, if you live to be yourself, to be settled in the world, or if you should gain an estate in it: but look upon it that you shall then be happy, when you can be constantly employed for God, and not for yourself; and desire to live in this world, only to do and suffer what God allots to you. . . .

"Once more; Never think that you can live to God by your own power or strength; but always look to, and rely on him for assistance, yea for all strength and grace. There is no greater truth than this, that 'we can do nothing of ourselves;' (John xv. 5. and 2 Cor. iii. 5.) yet nothing but our own experience can effectually teach us. Indeed we are a long time in learning, that all our strength and salvation, is in God." (pp. 124-25)

Prayer

O Lord, I do need guidelines to help me cultivate an effective life of prayer. May I become acquainted with the masters of the interior life and learn from them. Help me now to assimilate Brainerd's five simple rules into my own devotional discipline. Grant that I may be serious in my praying, prudent in the use of my time, conscious of my work as a sacred vocation; that I may center my happiness in your presence and above all depend not upon my own strength but upon your grace alone. Amen.

Adoration:
Alone with God

"Began to study the Indian tongue, with Mr. Sergeant at Stockbridge. Was perplexed for want of more retirement. I love to live alone in my own little cottage, where I can spend much time in prayer, &c." (p. 119)

"Was employed much of the day in writing; and spent some time in other necessary employment. But my time passes away so swiftly, that I am astonished when I reflect on it, and see how little I do. My state of solitude does not make the hours hang heavy upon my hands. O what reason of thankfulness have I on account of this retirement! I find, that I do not, and it seems I cannot lead a Christian life, when I am abroad, and cannot spend time in devotion, Christian conversation, and serious meditation, as I should do. Those weeks that I am obliged now to be home, in order to learn the Indian tongue, are mostly spent in perplexity and barrenness, without much sweet relish of divine things; and I feel myself a stranger at the throne of grace, for want of more frequent and continued retirement. When I return home, and give myself to meditation, prayer and fasting, a new scene opens to my mind, and my soul longs for mortification, self-denial, humility, and divorcement from all things of the world. This evening, my heart was somewhat warm and fervent in prayer and meditation, so that I was loth to indulge sleep. Continued in those duties till about midnight." (pp. 125-26)

"Spent this day in seriousness, with steadfast resolutions

for God, and a life of mortification. Studied closely, till I felt my bodily strength fail. . . . In the evening, though tired, was enabled to continue instant in prayer for some time. Spent the time in reading, meditation, and prayer, till the evening was far spent; was grieved to think that I could not watch unto prayer the whole night. But blessed be God, heaven is a place of continual and incessant devotion, though the earth is dull." (pp. 126-27)

Prayer
How creative, O God, are the moments spent along in your presence at the beginning of the day, at its close or at some other special time. Without these periods of inner renewal my soul becomes dry. Help me to use my solitude as a means whereby I can learn to adore you, through Christ my Lord. Amen.

Adoration: Communion with God

"Felt very sweetly, when I first rose in the morning. In family prayer, had some enlargement, but not much spirituality, till eternity came up before me, and looked near; I found some sweetness in the thoughts of bidding a dying farewell to this tiresome world. . . . Felt exceedingly weaned from the world to-day. In the afternoon, I discoursed on divine things, with a dear christian friend, whereby we were both refreshed. Then I prayed, with a sweet sense of the blessedness of communion with God: I think I scarce ever enjoyed more of God in any one prayer. O it was a blessed season indeed to my soul! I know not that ever I saw so much of my own nothingness, in my life; never wondered so, that God allowed me to preach his word. This has been a sweet and comfortable day to my soul. Blessed be God. Prayed again with my dear friend, with something of the divine presence. I long to be wholly conformed to God, and transformed into his image.

"Spent much of the day alone: enjoyed the presence of God in some comfortable degree: was visited by some dear friends, and prayed with them: wrote sundry letters to friends: felt religion in my soul while writing: enjoyed sweet meditations on some scriptures. . . .

"In the afternoon, prayed with a dear friend privately, and had the presence of God with us; our souls united together to reach after a blessed immortality, to be unclothed of the body of sin and death, and to enter the blessed world, where no unclean thing enters. O, with what intense desire did our souls long for that blessed day, that we might be freed from sin, and for ever live to and in our God! In the evening, took leave of that house; but first kneeled down and prayed; the Lord was of a truth in the midst of us; it was a sweet parting season; felt in myself much sweetness and affection in the things of God. Blessed be God for every such divine gale of his Spirit, to speed me on in my way to the new Jerusalem! Felt some sweetness afterwards, and spent the evening in conversation with friends, and prayed with some life, and retired to rest very late." (pp. 74-75)

"O, how delightful it is, to pray under such sweet influences! O, how much better is this, than one's necessary food! I had at this time no disposition to eat, (though late in the morning;) for earthly food appeared wholly tasteless. O how much 'better is thy love than wine,' than the sweetest wine!" (pp. 182-83)

Prayer

May I also enjoy such satisfying communion, O God. May your Spirit move me closer and closer into that deeper fellowship where I ask for nothing but yearn simply to be with you. Your love is indeed better than the sweetest wine. I pray in the name of Jesus, who knew this intimate communion best of all. Amen.

Confession:
Personal Unworthiness

"Saw so much of the wickedness of my heart, that I longed to get away from myself. I never before thought that there was so much spiritual pride in my soul. I felt almost pressed to death with my own vileness. O what a body of death is there in me! Lord, deliver my soul!" (p. 63)

"My soul is, and has for a long time been in a piteous condition, wading through a series of sorrows, of various kinds. I have been so crushed down sometimes with a sense of meanness and infinite unworthiness, that I have been ashamed that any, even the meanest of my fellow-creatures, should so much as spend a thought about me; and have wished sometimes, while travelling among the thick brakes, to drop, as one of them, into everlasting oblivion. In this case, sometimes, I have almost resolved never again to see any of my acquaintance: and really thought, I could not do it and hold up my face; and have longed for the remotest region, for a retreat from all my friends, that I might not be seen or heard of any more. Sometimes the consideration of my ignorance has been a means of my great distress and anxiety. And especially my soul has been in anguish with fear, shame, and guilt, that ever I had preached, or had any thought that way. —Sometimes my soul has been in distress on feeling some particular corruptions rise and swell like a mighty torrent, with present violence; having, at the same time, ten thousand former sins and follies presented to view, in all their blackness and aggravations. —And these, while destitute of most of the conveniences of life, and I may say, of all the pleasures of it; without a friend to communicate any of my sorrows to, and sometimes without any place of retirement, where I may unburden my soul before God, which has greatly contributed to my distress. —Of late, more especially, my great difficulty has been a sort of carelessness, a kind of regardless temper of mind, whence I have been disposed to indolence and trifling: and this temper of mind has constantly been attended with guilt and shame; so that sometimes I have been in a kind of horror, to find myself so unlike the blessed God. I have thought I grew worse under all my trials; and nothing has cut and wounded my soul more than this. O, if I am one of God's chosen, as I trust through infinite grace I am, I find of a truth, that the righteous are scarcely saved." (pp. 102-03)

Prayer

The brightness and holiness of your presence, O God, cause me to see myself as I really am. Too often I think more highly of myself than I should. Enable me through confession to purge myself of self-will and inordinate pride. O God, create in me a clean heart and renew a right spirit within me, through Christ my Lord. Amen.

Confession:
Past Mistakes

10 "Exceedingly depressed in spirit, it cuts and wounds my heart, to think how much self-exaltation, spiritual pride, and warmth of temper, I have formerly had intermingled with my endeavours to promote God's work; and sometimes I long to lie down at the feet of opposers, and confess what a poor imperfect creature I have been, and still am. The Lord forgive me, and make me for the future wise as a serpent, and harmless as a dove!" (p. 71)

"At night enjoyed much of God, in secret prayer: felt an uncommon resignation, to be and do what God pleased. Some days past, I felt great perplexity on account of past conduct: my bitterness, and want of a spirit of meekness!" (p. 76)

"In the morning, was in a devout, tender, and loving frame of mind; and was enabled to cry to God, I hope, with a childlike spirit, with importunity, resignation and composure of mind. My spirit was full of quietness, and love to mankind; and longed that peace should reign on the earth; was grieved at the very thoughts of a fiery, angry and intemperate zeal in religion; mourned over past follies in that regard; and confided in God for strength and grace sufficient for my future work and trials. Spent the day mainly in hard labour, making preparation for my intended journey." (p. 140)

"This morning, I was great oppressed with guilt and shame, from a sense of inward vileness and pollution. About nine, withdrew to the woods for prayer; but had not much comfort; I appeared to myself the vilest, meanest creature upon earth, and could scarcely live with myself; so mean and vile I appeared, that I thought I should never be able to hold my face in heaven, if God of his infinite grace should bring me thither." (p. 156)

Prayer

O Lord, help me to be specific in my confession. It is possible to be so general that I really miss the things that are blocking my communion with you and hindering my service to others. I too have made costly mistakes. I have spoken rashly. I have hurt my brother. I have been intemperate in my zeal. But, O Lord, in the process of bringing out my specific mistakes into the open, deliver me from being so overwhelmed by them that I become paralyzed in my efforts to serve you or my fellow man. Forgive me and set me free in the name of Christ, the Liberator. Amen.

Thanksgiving: God's Providence

"This day rode home to my own house and people. The poor Indians appeared very glad of my return. Found my house and all things in safety. I presently fell on my knees, and blessed God for my safe return, after a long and tedious journey, and a session of sickness in several places where I had been, and after I had been ill myself. God has renewed his kindness of me, in preserving me one journey more. I have taken many considerable journies since this time last year, and yet God has never suffered one of my bones to be broken, or any distressing calamity to befall me, excepting the ill turn I had in my last journey. I have been often exposed·to cold and hunger in the wilderness, where the comforts of life were not to be had; have frequently been lost in the woods; and sometimes obliged to ride much of the night; and once lay out in the woods all night; yet blessed be God, he has preserved me!" (p. 113)

"Rode home to the Forks of Delaware. What reason have I to bless God, who has preserved me in riding more than four hundred and twenty miles, and has 'kept all my bones, that not one of them has been broken!' My health likewise is greatly recovered. Oh that I could dedicate my all to God! This is all the return I can make to him." (p. 162)

"Spent most of the day in preparing for a journey to New England. Spent some time in prayer, with a special reference to my intended journey. Was afraid I should forsake the

Fountains of living waters, and attempt to derive satisfaction from broken cisterns, my dear friends and acquaintance, with whom I might meet in my journey. I looked to God to keep me from this vanity, as well as others. Towards night, and in the evening, was visited by some friends, some of whom, I trust, were real Christians; who discovered an affectionate regard to me, and seemed grieved that I was about to leave them; especially as I did not expect to make any considerable stay among them, if I should live to return from New England. O how kind has God been to me! how has he raised up friends in every place where his providence has called me! Friends are a great comfort; and it is God who gives them; it is He who makes them friendly to me. Bless the Lord, O my soul, and forget not all his benefits." (pp. 194-95)

Prayer

Instill in me, O God, a spirit of thanksgiving that shows appreciation for your providential care. How uncertain life is as I move along in my own journey. How easily it is for the best prepared plans to come to nothing. I thank you especially for my friends who are companions along the way. Surely these friends are gifts from your gracious hand. May I not take them for granted but ever praise you in the name of the one who laid down his life for his friends, even Jesus my Lord. Amen.

Thanksgiving: God's Power

12 "Went to the Indians, and discoursed to them near an hour, without any power to come close to their hearts. But at last, I felt some fervency, and God helped me speak with warmth. My Interpreter also was amazingly assisted; and I doubt not but that 'the Spirit of God was upon him;' and though I had had no reason to think he had any true and saving grace, but was only under conviction of his lost state; and presently upon this most of the grown persons were much affected, and the tears ran down their cheeks. One old man, I suppose an hundred years old, was so much affected, that he wept and seemed convinced of the importance of what I taught him. I staid with them a considerable time, exhorting and directing them; and came away, lifting up my heart to God in prayer and praise, and encouraged and exhorted my Interpreter to 'strive to enter at the strait gate,' Came home, and spent most of the evening in prayer and thanksgiving; and found myself much enlarged and quickened. Was greatly concerned, that the Lord's work which seemed to be begun, might be carried on with power, to the conversion of poor souls, and the glory of divine grace." (pp. 184-85)

"Spent a great part of the day in prayer to God for the outpouring of his Spirit on my poor people; as also to bless his name for awakening my Interpreter and some others, and giving us some tokens of his presence yesterday. And blessed be God, I had much freedom, five or six times in the day, in prayer and praise, and felt a weighty concern upon my spirit for the salvation of those precious souls, and the enlargement of the Redeemer's kingdom among them. My soul hoped in God for some success in my ministry: and blessed be his name for so much hope." (p. 185)

"In the morning, God was pleased to remove that gloom which has of late oppressed my mind, and gave me freedom and sweetness in prayer. I was encouraged, strengthened, and enabled to plead for grace for myself, and mercy for my poor Indians; and was sweetly assisted in my intercessions with God for others. Blessed be his holy name for ever and ever. Amen, and Amen. Those things that of late appeared most difficult and almost impossible, now appeared not only possible, but easy. My soul was much delighted to continue instant in prayer, at this blessed season, that I had no desire for my necessary food: even dreaded leaving off praying at all, lest I should lose this spirituality, and this blessed thankfulness to God which I then felt." (pp. 188-89)

Prayer
Almighty and gracious God, I praise you for the varied manifestations of your power. I have experienced your power in my own life and have observed it in the lives of other people. Grant that such evidence, even when it appears limited and spasmodic, will fill me with hope to expect greater things in the future, in Jesus' name. Amen.

Petition: To Be More Holy

13 "I wished and longed for the coming of my dear Lord: I longed to join the angelic hosts in praises, wholly free from imperfection. O, the blessed moment hastens! All I want is to be more holy, more like my dear Lord." (p. 59)

"In times past, he has given me inexpressible sweetness in the performance of duty. Frequently my soul has enjoyed much of God; . . . But of late, God has been pleased to keep my soul hungry, almost continually; so that I have been filled with a kind of pleasing pain. When I really enjoy God, I feel my desires of him the more insatiable, and my thirstings after holiness the more unquenchable; and the Lord will not allow me to feel as though I were fully supplied and satisfied, but keeps me still reaching forward. I feel barren and empty, as though I could not live, without more of God; I feel ashamed and guilty before him. I see that 'the law is spiritual, but I am carnal,' I do not, I cannot live to God. Oh for holiness! Oh for more of God in my soul! Oh this pleasing pain! It makes my soul press after God; the language of it is, 'Then shall I be satisfied, when I awake in God's likeness,' but never, never before: and consequently, I am engaged to 'press towards the mark,' day by day. Oh that I may feel this continual hunger, and not be retarded, but rather animated by every cluster from Canaan, to reach forward in the narrow way, for the full enjoyment and possession of the heavenly inheritance! Oh that I may never loiter in my heavenly journey!" (p. 80)

"At noon, I longed for sanctification, and conformity to God. O that is THE ALL, THE ALL. The Lord help me to press after God for ever." (p. 80)

"Spent most of the day in writing. Enjoyed some sense of religion. Through divine goodness I am now uninterruptedly alone; and find my retirement comfortable. . . . I longed after holiness, humility and meekness: Oh that God would enable me to 'pass the time of my sojourning here in his fear,' and always live to him!" (p. 104)

Prayer

Do I have a "pleasing pain" that compels me to seek after you, O God? Do I press after that deeper experience of knowing you, of becoming more like you? Or have I settled complacently upon a plateau on my journey and no longer have the will to climb to higher reaches? O God, may my cry be: "Oh for holiness! Oh for more of God in my soul!" Amen.

Petition:
Unity and Harmony

"In the morning, continued still in perplexity. —In the evening enjoyed comfort sufficient to overbalance all my late distresses. I saw that God is the only soul-satisfying portion, and I really found satisfaction in him. My soul was much enlarged in sweet intercession for my fellow-men every where, and for many Christian friends in particular, in distant places." (p. 72)

"Preached to a pretty large assembly . . . insisted on humility and steadfastness in keeping God's commands: and that through humility we should prefer one another in love, and not make our own frames the rule by which we judge others. I felt sweetly calm, and full of brotherly love; and never more free from party spirit. I hope some good will follow; that Christians will be freed from false joy, and party zeal, and censuring one another." (p. 89)

"Studied in the forenoon, and enjoyed some freedom. . . . In evening prayer, God was pleased to draw near to my soul, though very sinful and unworthy; so that I was enabled to wrestle with God, and to persevere in my requests for grace. I poured out my soul for all the world, friends, and enemies. My soul was concerned, not so much for souls as such, but rather for Christ's kingdom, that it might appear in the world, that God might be known to be God, in the whole earth. And O my soul abhorred the very thought of a party in religion! Let the truth of God appear, wherever it is; and God have the glory for ever. Amen." (p. 107)

Prayer

O Lord, remove the divisive spirit from my heart. May I be slow to judge and censure others. May I pray for coworkers whose styles are different from my own. May I pray for those who personally attack me. Draw me close in fellowship to all those who claim allegiance to Christ. We are indeed one in the Spirit as Christians; help me to do my own part in making this inherent unity more visible in my own sphere of influence, in the name and for the sake of Christ, who prayed that we might all be one. Amen.

Petition: Ordained to Serve

15 "At Newark in the morning was much concerned how I should perform the work of the day; and trembled at the thoughts of being left to myself. Enjoyed very considerable assistance in all parts of the public service. Had an opportunity again to attend on the ordinance of the Lord's supper, and through divine goodness was refreshed in it: my soul was full of love and tenderness towards the children of God, and towards all men; felt a certain sweetness of disposition towards every creature. At night, I enjoyed more spirituality and sweet desire of holiness, than I have felt for some time: was afraid of every thought and every motion, lest thereby my heart should be drawn away from God. Oh that I might never leave the blessed God! 'Lord in thy presence is fulness of joy.' O the blessedness of living to God!

"This day the Presbytery met together at Newark, in order to my ordination. Was very weak and disordered in body; yet endeavoured to repose my confidence in God. Spent most of the day alone; especially the forenoon. At three in the afternoon preached my probation sermon from Acts xxvi. 17, 18. 'Delivering thee from the people, and from the Gentiles, &c.' being a text given me for that end. Felt not well either in body; however, God carried me through comfortably. Afterwards, passed an examination before the Presbytery. Was much tired, and my mind burdened with the greatness of that charge I was in the most solemn manner about to take upon me: my mind was so pressed with the weight of the work incumbent upon me, that I could not sleep this night, though very weary and in great need of rest.

"Was this morning further examined, respecting my experimental acquaintance with christianity. At ten o'clock my ordination was attended; the sermon preached by the Rev. Mr. Pemberton. At this time I was affected with a sense of the important trust committed to me; yet was composed, and solemn, without distraction; and I hope that then, as many times before, I gave myself up to God, to be for him, and not for another. Oh that I might always be engaged in the service of God, and duly remember the solemn charge I have received, in the presence of God, angels, and men. Amen. May I be assisted of God for this purpose." (pp. 147-48)

Prayer

O God, you set apart certain people in your church to serve in specific functions. Those of us who serve in the ministry of the Word, whether in a gathered congregation or in a peripatetic mission, need your grace to fulfill our tasks. What a serious responsibility it is to be set apart by prayer and the laying on of hands for a special assignment. May I not forget the solemn charge that I personally have in the church of Jesus Christ, in whose name I pray. Amen.

Intercession: Empathy for the Indians

16 "In the morning, was perplexed with wandering vain thoughts; was much grieved, judged and condemned myself before God. O how miserable did I feel, because I could not live to God! At ten, rode away with a heavy heart, to preach to my Indians. Upon the road I attempted to lift up my heart to God; but was infested with an unsettled wandering frame of mind; and was exceeding restless and perplexed, and filled with shame and confusion before God. I seemed to myself to be 'more brutish than any man;' and though none deserved to be 'cast out of God's presence' so much as I. If I attempted to lift up my heart to God, as I frequently did by the way, on a sudden, before I was aware, my thoughts were wandering 'to the ends of the earth;' and my soul was filled with surprise and anxiety, to find it thus. . . . after I came to the Indians, my mind was confused; and I felt nothing sensibly of that sweet reliance on God, with which my soul has been comforted in days past. Spent the forenoon in this posture of mind, and preached to the Indians without any heart. In the afternoon, I felt still barren, when I began to preach, and for about half an hour. I seemed to myself to know nothing, and to have nothing to say to the Indians; but soon after, I found in myself a spirit of love, and warmth, and power, to address the poor Indians; and God helped me to plead with them, to turn from all the vanities of the Heathen, to the living God; I am persuaded that the Lord touched their consciences; for I never saw such attention raised in them. When I came away from them, I spent the whole time while I was riding to my lodgings, three miles distant, in prayer and praise to God. After I had rode more than two miles, it came into my mind to dedicate myself to God again; which I did with great solemnity and unspeakable satisfaction; especially gave up myself to him renewedly in the work of the ministry. This I did by divine grace, I hope, without any exception or reserve; not in the least shrinking back from any difficulties that might attend this great and blessed work. I seemed to be most free, cheerful, and full in this dedication of myself. My whole soul cried 'Lord, to thee I dedicate myself! O accept of me, and let me be thine for ever. Lord, I desire nothing else; I desire nothing more.'...

"My heart rejoiced in my particular work as a missionary; rejoiced in my necessity of self-denial in many respects; and still continued to give up myself to God, and implore mercy of him, praying incessantly, every moment, with sweet fervency." (pp. 152-53)

Prayer

Eternal God, teach me how to intercede for others. Grant me empathy to view things from the other side. May I learn to sit where other people sit. Help me in particular to identify with the red, black, brown and yellow peoples of the world and see things as they see them. Infuse me with the universality of Jesus' compassion. May I be immersed in such love so that I will be able to love as I ought to love. Amen.

Intercession: Prosperity of His Mission

17 "Awoke this morning in the fear of God: soon called to mind my sadness in the evening past; and spent my first waking minutes in prayer for sanctification, that my soul may be washed from its exceeding pollution and defilement. After I arose, I spent some time in reading God's word and in prayer. I cried to God under a sense of my great indigence.... Last year, I longed to be prepared for a world of glory, and speedily to depart out of this world; but of late all my concern almost is for the conversion of the Heathen; and for that end I long to live. But blessed be God, I have less desire to live for any of the pleasures of the world, that I ever had. I long and love to be a pilgrim; and want more grace to imitate the life, labours and sufferings of St. Paul among the Heathen. And when I long for holiness now, it is not so much for myself as formerly; but rather that thereby I may become an 'able minister of the New-Testament.' " (p. 154)

"I love to be a pilgrim and stranger in this wilderness; it seems most fit for such a poor, ignorant, worthless, despised creature as I. I would not change my present mission for any other business in the whole world. I may tell you freely, without vanity and ostentation, God has of late given me great freedom and fervency in prayer, when I have been so weak and feeble that my nature seemed as if it would speedily dissolve. I feel as if my all was lost, and I was undone for this world, if the poor Heathen may not be converted. I feel, in general, different from what I did, when I saw you last; at least more crucified to all the enjoyments of life. It would be very refreshing to me to see you here in this desert; especially in my weak disconsolate hours; but, I think, I could be content never to see you, or any of my friends again in this world, if God would bless my labours here to the conversion of the poor Indians." (p. 160—excerpt from a letter to a close friend)

Prayer

O Lord, unless your Spirit is at work in my personal witness all is in vain. Therefore, I pray that your Spirit will continue to motivate me in my mission. Teach me to pray like Brainerd and give me a consuming passion to fulfill my calling even as he fulfilled his calling, through Jesus Christ my Lord. Amen.

III
THE DARK NIGHT
OF THE SOUL

Cranberry, New Jersey,
where Brainerd shared life with the Indians.

"In the former part of his religious course, he imputed much of that kind of gloominess of mind, and those dark thoughts, to spiritual desertion which in the latter part of his life he was abundantly sensible were owing to the disease of melancholy."[1]

Jonathan Edwards

Sooner or later those who take seriously the devotional life encounter the "dark night of the soul." It is often referred to as spiritual dryness or a "mystic death." Contact with God is negligible. Acute depression settles in. It is not just the sensation of marking time in devotional discipline but rather of losing ground, or having less of an awareness of God than when the journey first began.

John of the Cross, the Spanish mystic who gave classic definition to the term "dark night of the soul" in his work by the same name, was convinced that the "dark night" was a prelude to a keener perception of the Divine Light.

In John's own words,
"O Happy night and blest!
Secretly speeding, screen'd from mortal gaze,
Unseeing, on I prest,
Lit by no earthly rays,
Nay, only by heart's inmost fire ablaze."[2]

The "dark night" can be interpreted not only as preparation for seeing God more clearly but also as equipping us for more effective mission. Frank Laubach, the apostle to the illiterate people of the world, wrote of his own "dark night" in Mindanao, the Philippines, when, in 1930, he realized he was failing as a missionary. Out of his despair he surrendered anew his life to God, and he received, in his own words, "a tender compassion for the multitudes which has been the driving power of my life ever since."[3]

Edwards had high praise for the enduring quality of Brainerd's devotional life and reflected, "His religion was not like a blazing meteor, or like a flaming comet . . . flying through the firmament with a bright train, and then quickly departing into perfect darkness; but more like the steady lights of heaven, constant principles of light, though sometimes hid with clouds."[4] But Brainerd's spiritual journey before his great awakening was a continual alternation between faith and doubt, between assurance and despair. The "clouds" referred to by Edwards were the extended periods of depression that he endured from his youth. He had to struggle with his spirit of melancholy that threatened at times to overpower him.

Probably the darkest moment in Brainerd's own mission occurred in the summer of 1745. He had been laboring for about a year among the Delaware and Susquehanna Indians. But, as one of his biographers comments, "He was a lone voice crying in the wilderness and the passers-by, though curious, gave scant heed to his crying. His year in Penn's Woods seemed a complete failure."[5]

The following selections isolate a number of the principal

factors that contributed to Brainerd's "dark night of the soul." Among these were his loneliness, his chronic illness, his melancholy spirit, his ineffective ministry and, worst of all, the absence of God. Analyzing his crisis should be useful to us in comprehending and hopefully in overcoming the "dark night" when it arrives in our own devotional quest.

The Loneliness of the Journey

18 "My circumstances are such, that I have no comfort of any kind, but what I have in God. I live in the most lonesome wilderness; have but one single person to converse with that can speak English. Most of talk I hear, is either Highland Scotch, or Indian. I have no fellow-Christian to whom I may ... lay open my spiritual sorrows; with whom I may take sweet counsel in conversation about heavenly things, and join in social prayer. I live poorly with regard to the comforts of life; most of my diet consists of boiled corn, hasty-pudding, &c. I lodge on a bundle of straw, my labour is ... extremely difficult, and I have little appearance of success, to comfort me. The Indians have no land to live on, but what the Dutch people lay claim to; and these threaten to drive them off. They have no regard to the souls of the poor Indians; and by what I can learn, they hate me because I come to preach to them. But that which makes all my difficulties grievous to be borne, is, that God hides his face from me." (p. 101)

"Was very much disordered with a cold and pain in my head. About six at night, I lost my way in the wilderness, and wandered over rocks and mountains, down hideous steeps, through swamps, and most dreadful and dangerous places; and, the night being dark, so that few stars could be seen, I was greatly exposed. I was much pinched with cold, and distressed with an extreme pain in my head, attended with sickness at my stomach; so that every step I took was distressing to me. I had little hope for several hours together, but that I must lie out in the woods all night, in this distressed case.... In this world I expect tribulation; and it does not now, as formerly, appear strange to me. I do not in such seasons of difficulty flatter myself that it will be better hereafter; but rather think how much worse it might be; how much greater trials others of God's children have endured; and how much greater are yet perhaps reserved for me." (pp. 179-80)

"Was scarce able to walk about, and was obliged to betake myself to bed, much of the day; and passed away the time in a very solitary manner; being neither able to read, meditate, nor pray, and had none to converse with in that wilderness. O how heavily does time pass away, when I can do nothing to any good purpose; but seem obliged to trifle away precious time!" (p. 197)

Prayer

O Lord, deliver me from the darkness of my loneliness. Your call beckons me to venture forth along unknown paths where I would not ordinarily go, and sometimes the journey becomes lonely. Strengthen me in such moments of desolation with your peace so that I may trust that you are present with me even though you are present in a way I cannot fully comprehend, in Jesus' name. Amen.

Chronic Illness

19 "Had thoughts of going forward on my journey to my Indians; but towards night was taken with a hard pain in my teeth, and shivering cold; and could not possibly recover a comfortable degree of warmth the whole night following. I continued very full of pain all night; and in the morning had a very hard fever, and pains almost over my whole body. I had a sense of the divine goodness in appointing this to be the place of my sickness, among my friends who were very kind to me.... Here, I saw, was mercy in the midst of affliction. I continued, thus, mostly confined to my bed, till Friday night; very full of pain most of the time; but through divine goodness, not afraid of death. Then the extreme folly of those appeared to me, who put off their turning to God till a sick bed. Surely this is not a time proper to prepare for eternity." (pp. 112-13)

"Was very much disordered in body, and sometimes full of pain in my face and teeth; was not able to study much, and had not much spiritual comfort. Alas! when God is withdrawn, all is gone." (p. 116)

"Enjoyed not so much health of body, or fervour of mind, as yesterday. If the chariot-wheels move with ease and speed at any time, for a short space; yet by and by they drive heavily again. 'Oh that I had the wings of a dove, that I might fly away' from sin and corruption, and be at rest with God!" (p. 119)

Prayer

O Lord, deliver me from the darkness of chronic illness. It is difficult to understand why some people suffer as they do; they often seem to be the best people I know. Grant that I may have greater appreciation for their misery. Help me to deal creatively with my own illness. Prevent me from becoming bitter and estranged from your will. Bless all physicians, nurses, researchers and others in the field of medical science who work to alleviate physical suffering. I pray in the name of Jesus, whose very name signifies salvation, wholeness and health. Amen.

Clouds of Melancholy

20 "Though very weak, I visited and preached to the poor Indians twice, and was strengthened vastly beyond my expectations. Indeed, the Lord gave me some freedom and fervency in addressing them; though I had not strength enough to stand, but was obliged to sit down the whole time. Towards night, was extremely weak, faint, sick, and full of pain. I have continued much in the same state I was in last week, though most of this, (it being now Friday,) unable to engage in any business; frequently unable to pray in the family. I am obliged to let all my thoughts and concerns run at random; for I have not strength to read, meditate, or pray: and this naturally perplexes my mind.

"I seem to myself like a man that has all his estate embarked in one small boat, unhappily going adrift, down a swift torrent. The poor owner stands on the shore, and looks, and laments his loss—But alas! though my all seems to be adrift, and I stand and see it, I dare not lament; for this sinks my spirits more, and aggravates my bodily disorders! I am forced therefore to divert myself with trifles; although at the same time I am afraid, and often feel as I was guilty of the misimprovement of time. And oftentimes my conscience is so exercised, with this miserable way of spending time, that I have no peace; though I have no strength of mind or body to improve it to better purpose. Oh that God would pity my distressed state!" (pp. 160-61)

"Was so overwhelmed with dejection that I knew not how to live. I longed for death exceedingly: my soul was sunk into deep waters, and the floods were ready to drown me. I was so much oppressed, that my soul was in a kind of horror; could not keep my thoughts fixed in prayer, for the space of one minute, without fluttering and distraction; and was exceedingly ashamed, that I did not live to God." (p. 184)

Prayer

O Lord, deliver me from the darkness of melancholy. Often the maladies of the mind are more severe than the maladies of the body. There is some consolation in knowing that many of the most sensitive saints who have traveled the pathways of the inner life have also endured doubt, depression and despair. When the clouds of melancholy surround me, O Lord, and blur my vision, sharpen my memory to recall those times when your presence was luminously clear and grant me patience to believe that when these clouds of melancholy which presently engulf me eventually move away I will behold your gracious presence once again. I pray in the name of Jesus, who is the light of the world. Amen.

An Ineffective Ministry

21 "I scarce ever felt myself so unfit to exist as now: saw I was not worthy of a place among the Indians, where I am going, if God permit: thought I should be ashamed to look them in the face, and much more to have any respect shewn me there. Indeed I felt myself banished from the earth, as if all places were too good for such a wretch. . . . I appeared to myself a creature fit for nothing, neither heaven nor earth." (pp. 88-89)

"Was somewhat better in health than of late; and was able to spend a considerable part of the day in prayer and close study. Had more freedom and fervency in prayer than usual of late; especially longed for the presence of God in my work. . . . And in evening prayer my faith and hope in God were much raised. To an eye of reason every thing that respects the conversion of the Heathen is as dark as midnight; and yet I cannot but hope in God for the accomplishment of something glorious among them. My soul longed much for the advancement of the Redeemer's kingdom on earth." (p. 150)

"Had the greatest degree of inward anguish which I almost ever endured. I was perfectly overwhelmed, and so confused, that after I began to discourse to the Indians, before I could finish a sentence, sometimes I forgot entirely what I was aiming at; or if, with much difficulty, I had recollected what I had before designed, still it appeared strange, and like something which I had long forgotten, and had now but an imperfect remembrance of. I know it was a degree of distraction, occasioned by . . . melancholy, spiritual desertion, and some other things that particularly pressed upon me this morning, with an uncommon weight, the principal of which respected my Indians. This distressing gloom never went off the whole day; . . . In the evening this gloom continued, till family prayer, about nine o'clock." (p. 190)

Prayer

O Lord, deliver me from the darkness of an ineffective ministry. No one ever likes to fail, and yet so often the response to our personal witness is slight. Help me to believe that even when the situation appears to be as "dark as midnight" I can still trust you and believe that the dawn will eventually come. Amen.

The Absence of God

22 "My spiritual conflicts to-day were unspeakably dreadful, heavier than the mountains and over-flowing floods. I seemed inclosed, as it were, in hell itself: I was deprived of all sense of God, even of the being of a God; and this was my misery.... This taught me the absolute dependence of a creature upon God the Creator, for every crumb of happiness it enjoys. Oh I feel that, if there is no God, though I might live for ever here, and enjoy not only this, but all other worlds, I should be ten thousand times more miserable than a reptile. My soul was in such anguish I could not eat; but felt as I suppose a poor wretch would that is just going to the place of execution." (pp. 87-88)

"O my soul, what death it is, to have the affections unable to centre in God, by reason of darkness, and consequent roving after that satisfaction elsewhere, that is only to be found here!" (p. 164)

"Was sensible of my barrenness and decays in the things of God: my soul failed when I remembered the fervency which I had enjoyed at the throne of grace. O, I thought, if I could but be spiritual, warm, heavenly-minded, and affectionately breathing after God, this would be better than life to me! My soul longed exceedingly for death, to be loosed from this dullness and barrenness, and made for ever active in the service of God. I seemed to live for nothing, and to do no good: and O, the burden of such a life! O death, death, my kind friend, hasten, and deliver me from dull mortality, and make me spiritual and vigorous to eternity!" (p. 167)

"None know, but those who feel it, what the soul endures that is sensibly shut out from the presence of God: alas! it is more bitter than death." (p. 89)

Prayer

O Lord, deliver me from the darkness of your absence. This is the worst darkness of all. Almost anything else is bearable, except to be separated from your presence. Help me to probe the experience of Jesus in the Garden of Gethsemane and upon the cross. May I view his dereliction from the brightness of Easter morning. Help me to identify also with Brainerd, your servant, and the anguish of his "dark night" when he sensed he was isolated from your presence. As I recall that his darkest moment was shortly followed by a great awakening, may I commit all things into your hands. In my own darkness may I trust that you will lead me through the night until I walk in the sunlight once again, in Jesus' name. Amen.

IV

THE GREAT
AWAKENING

Crossweeksung, now Crosswicks, New Jersey,
where Brainerd experienced his first major success.

"Let every preacher read carefully over the life of David Brainerd. Let us be followers of him, as he was of Christ, in absolute self-devotion, in total deafness to the world and in fervent love to God and man."[1]

John Wesley, leader of England's evangelical revival and founder of Methodism

The Great Awakening is an apt term to describe the fourth stage in Brainerd's spiritual journey. In some respects his awakening was similar to the stage of illumination in the mystic quest—a time of knowing the intimacy of God's presence, of happiness, perhaps even of ecstasy and of freedom to do God's will.[2] Brainerd's own awakening enabled him to conquer his melancholy spirit, gave him a sense of spiritual assurance and above all else equipped him to be an instrument in bringing the awakening to others. To him the all-important objective was not a heightened subjective awareness of God's presence but rather the attainment of liberty to be an effective servant in glorifying God.

Brainerd's personal illumination must be viewed in the larger context of the Great Awakening that permeated colonial America beginning as early as 1720. Among the leaders of America's first popular revival were Theodore Frelinghuysen, Gilbert Tennent, Jonathan Edwards and George Whitefield. All of these men called upon the people within and without the churches to move beyond intellectual and theoretical religious knowledge to a personal heartwarming encounter with Christ. In the wake of the emphasis upon individual conversion, fresh vitality surged through the churches, educational institutions were formed and an interest in missions to the Indians was renewed and expanded. Paradoxically, the Great Awakening had both unitive and divisive results. On the one hand, colonial and denominational barriers were overcome as never before. On the other hand, the Dutch Reformed, Presbyterian and Congregationalist churches were split into pro- and anti-revivalist factions.[3]

Brainerd first made contact with the revival when he was a student at Yale College, but it was not until the year which extended from the summer of 1745 to the summer of 1746 that he experienced the Awakening in its most exhilarating manner. Just when he had reached the conclusion that he was a failure as a missionary and was ready to return home so as not to waste the money of his supporters, the commissioners of the Society in Scotland for Propagating Christian Knowledge, he learned of Indians living in New Jersey. Instead of traveling westward toward the Susquehanna Valley as he had done before, this time he left the Forks of the Delaware and traveled eastward and came to a place called Crossweeksung in the area of Trenton and Freehold. Here he was startled at the immediate response of the Indians to the proclamation of the Christian message. A variety of Indians—young and old, men and women, and even a powwow or witch doctor—embraced the good news with ardent emotion. More than a hundred Indians at a time came to hear him preach during his stay in this region.

Cautious to avoid the excesses of the revival Brainerd brought a balanced approach to his missionary evangelism, appealing to the reason as well as to the emotions and will. An indigenous Indian church was organized providing Christian nurture in the form of worship, fellowship, study and discipline. He was also quick to recognize the social implications of his mission. When it became evident that the Indians' land was threatened at Crossweeksung, Brainerd urged his missionary society to raise additional money and secure adequate land. Cranberry was the site chosen for the new Indian community. At Cranberry abundant space was available for planting crops and hunting. In addition, a church, a school, a carpenter shop and an infirmary were soon constructed. These Indians and Brainerd shared life together and developed a unique and intimate Christian church.

Brainerd now reached the plateau of intense mystical communion with God that he had yearned for through the earlier years of his missionary travels, and, in his words, he wished "to burn out in one continued flame for God."[4] At last he had the satisfaction of seeing God's glory manifested in his work.

The ten selections in this fourth section are samples of Brainerd's observations and reflections upon the phenomenal year in his mission to the Indians. The reader will note the striking parallels between the issues of the first Great Awakening and the awakening of our own day. The first two selections remind us that the powerful working of God's Spirit appears at the least expected places and in the most extraordinary ways. The next four selections assist us in distinguishing between a genuine awakening and its artificial counterpart. Today, we must still underscore the supreme appeal of love, the centrality of Christ, the superiority of grace over the law and the need to go beyond mere emotionalism. The final four selections refer to the communal responsibilities of the pilgrim of the inner life. These obligations include corporate worship, an intimate sharing fellowship, a social conscience and an appreciation for the rich diversity and the essential unity of God's people.

The Journey's Surprising Turn

 "It is remarkable that God began this work among the Indians at a time when I had the least hope, and to my apprehension the least rational prospect of seeing a work of grace propagated among them: my bodily strength being then much wasted by a late tedious journey to the Susquehannah, where I was necessarily exposed to hardships and fatigues among the Indians: my mind being also exceedingly depressed with a view of the unsuccessfulness of my labours. I had little reason so much as to hope that God had made me instrumental in the saving conversion of any of the Indians, except my interpreter and his wife. Hence I was ready to look upon myself as a burden to the honourable Society which employed and supported me in this business, and began to entertain serious thoughts of giving up my mission; and almost resolved I would do so at the conclusion of the present year, if I had then no better prospect of special success in my work than I had hitherto had. I cannot say that I entertained these thoughts because I was weary of the labours and fatigues which necessarily attended my present business, or because I had light and freedom in my own mind to turn any other way; but purely through dejection of spirit, pressing discouragement, and apprehension of its being unjust to spend money consecrated to religious uses, only to civilize the Indians, and bring them to an external profession of Christianity. . . .

"In this frame of mind I first visited these Indians at Crossweeksung; apprehending that it was my indispensable duty, seeing I had heard there was a number in these parts, to make some attempts for their conversion to God, though I cannot say, I had any hope of success, my spirits being now so extremely sunk. I do not know that my hopes respecting the conversion of the Indians were ever reduced to so low an ebb, since I had any special concern for them, at this time. Yet this was the very season in which God saw fit to begin this glorious work! Thus he 'ordained strength out of weakness,' by making bare his almighty arm at a time when all hopes and human probabilities most evidently appeared to fail. —Whence I learn, that it is good to follow the path of duty, though in the midst of darkness and discouragement." (pp. 245-46)

Prayer

God of the future, you have promised to be with me on my journey, but I often have difficulty sensing your presence. I too at times am ready to give up and retrace my steps. Grant me patience to await your disclosure which may come when I have "least hope." Grant me perception to be alert to receive the surprises of your grace. And grant me perseverance because I may be on the verge of a great awakening, through Christ Jesus my Lord. Amen.

An Extraordinary Day

"In the afternoon I preached to the Indians, their number was now about sixty-five persons; men, women and children. I discoursed upon Luke 14, 16-23, and was favored with uncommon freedom in my discourse. There was much visible concern among them, while I was discoursing publicly; but afterwards, when I spoke to one and another more particularly, whom I perceived under much concern, the power of God seemed to descend upon the assembly 'like a mighty rushing wind,' and with an astonishing energy bore down all before it. I stood amazed at the influence, which seized the audience almost universally; and could compare it to nothing more aptly, than the irresistible force of a mighty torrent or swelling deluge, that with its insupportable weight and pressure bears down and sweeps before it whatever comes in its way. Almost all persons of all ages were bowed down with concern together, and scarcely one was able to withstand the shock of this surprising operation. Old men and women, who had been drunken wretches for many years, and some little children, not more than six or seven years of age, appeared in distress for their souls, as well as persons of middle age. . . . A principal man among the Indians, who before was the most secure and self-righteous, and thought his state good, because he knew more than the generality of the Indians had formerly done; and who with a great degree of confidence the day before told me 'he had been a Christian more than ten years;' was now brought under solemn concern for his soul, and wept bitterly. Another man advanced in years, who had been a murderer, a pawaw or conjurer, and a notorious drunkard, was likewise brought now to cry for mercy with many tears, and to complain much that he could be no more concerned when he saw his dangers so very great.

"They were almost universally praying and crying for mercy in every part of the house, and many out of doors; and numbers could neither go nor stand. Their concern was so great, each one for himself, that none seemed to take notice of those about them, but each prayed freely for himself. I am led to think they were, to their own apprehensions, as much retired as if they had been individually by themselves, in the thickest desert; or I believe rather that they thought nothing about any thing but themselves, and their own state, and so were every one praying apart, although all together. It seemed to me that there was now an exact fulfilment of that prophecy Zech. 12th, 10, 11, 12; for there was now 'a great mourning, like the mourning of Hadadrimmon;' and each seemed to 'mourn apart.' Methought this had a near resemblance to the day of God's power, mentioned Josh. 10th, 14; for I must say I never saw any day like it, in all respects: it was a day wherein I am persuaded the Lord did much to destroy the kingdom of darkness among this people." (pp. 218-19)

Prayer

O God of power, I praise you for the privilege of living in the midst of one of your extraordinary days. I see the signs of the awakening all about me—in the general thirst for transcendence, in the transformed lives of youth and young adults and in the rise of candidates for the Christian ministry. Keep me open to your moments of kairos when something really new can happen and enable me to celebrate joyfully the powerful presence of your Spirit, in the name of Christ. Amen.

The Supreme
Appeal of Love

25 "In the morning I discoursed to the Indians at the house where we lodged. Many of them were much affected, and appeared surprisingly tender; so that a few words about the concerns of their souls would cause the tears to flow freely, and produce many sobs and groans. In the afternoon, they being returned to the place where I had usually preached among them, I again discoursed to them.... There were about fifty-five persons in all; about forty that were capable of attending Divine service with understanding. I insisted on I John, 4th, 10th. 'Herein is love, &c.' They seemed eager of hearing; but there appeared nothing very remarkable, except their attention, till near the close of my discourse; and then Divine truths were attended with a surprising influence, and produced a great concern among them. There were scarcely three in forty who could refrain from tears and bitter cries. They all as one seemed in agony of soul to obtain an interest in Christ; and the more I discoursed of the love and compassion of God·in sending his Son to suffer for the sins of men; and the more I invited them to come and partake of his love; the more their distress was aggravated, because they felt themselves unable to come. It was surprising to see how their hearts seemed to be pierced with the tender and melting invitations of the gospel, when there was not a word of terror spoken to them." (p. 217)

"It is further remarkable, that God has carried on his work

here by such means, and in such a manner, as tended to obviate, and leave no room for, those prejudices and objections which have often been raised against such a work. When persons have been awakened to a solemn concern for their souls, by hearing the more awful truths of God's word, and the terrors of the divine law insisted upon, it has usually in such cases been objected by some, that such persons were only frightened with a fearful noise of hell and damnation; and that there was no evidence that their concern was the effect of a divine influence. But God has left no room for this objection in the present case; this work of grace having been begun and carried on, by almost one continued strain of gospel invitation to perishing sinners. This may reasonably be guessed, from a view of the passages of scripture I chiefly insisted upon in my discourses from time to time; which I have for that purpose inserted in my Diary." (pp. 249-50)

"This great awakening, this surprising concern, was never excited by any harangues of terror, but always appeared most remarkable when I insisted upon the compassion of a dying Saviour, the plentiful provisions of the gospel, and the free offers of divine grace, to needy, distressed sinners." (p. 250)

Prayer

Gracious God, in Jesus of Nazareth you have shown in word and deed that there is only one method to use in bearing witness to your glory—the way of love. Free me from all temptations to substitute coercion, deception or the latest gimmick in order to win the allegiance of others to Christ. May I not only proclaim the good news about Christ but proclaim it in the same spirit he exhibited. Amen.

The Centrality of Christ

"I cannot but take notice, that I have in general, ever since my first coming among the Indians in New-Jersey, been favoured with that assistance, which to me, is uncommon, in preaching Christ crucified, and making him the centre and mark to which all my discourses among were directed.

"It was the principal scope and drift of all my discourses to this people, for several months together, (after having taught them something of the being and perfections of God, his creation of man in a state of rectitude and happiness, and the obligations mankind were thence under to love and honour him,) to lead them into an acquaintance with their deplorable state by nature, as fallen creatures; their inability to extricate and deliver themselves from it; the utter insufficiency of any external reformations and amendments of life, or of any religious performances, of which they were capable, while in this state, to bring them into the favour of God, and interest them in his eternal mercy; thence to show them their absolute need of Christ to redeem and save them from the misery of their fallen state; to open his all-sufficiency and willingness to save the chief of sinners; the freeness and riches of divine grace, proposed 'without money and without price,' to all that will accept the offer.... These things, I repeatedly and largely insisted upon from time to time.

"I have oftentimes remarked with admiration, that whatever subject I have been treating upon, after having spent time sufficient to explain and illustrate the truths contained therein, I have been naturally and easily led to Christ as the substance of every subject. If I treated on the being and glorious perfections of God; I was thence naturally led to discourse of Christ as the only 'way to the Father.' If I attempted to open the deplorable misery of our fallen state; it was natural from thence to show the necessity of Christ to undertake for us, to atone for our sins, and to redeem us from the power of them. If I taught the commands of God and showed our violation of them; this brought me in the most easy and natural way, to speak of, and recommend the Lord Jesus Christ, as one who had 'magnified the law' which we had broken, and who was 'become the end of it for righteousness, to every one that believes.' Never did I find so much freedom and assistance in making all the various lines of my discourses meet together, and centre in Christ, as I have frequently done among these Indians." (pp. 321-22)

Prayer
Lord God Almighty, may all my prayers, thoughts and witness converge in exalting Christ. Surely my faith is centered not in an abstraction nor in an institution but in a person. Rid me of all sectarianism, vested interests and divisive speculations. Bring me back again and again to the primary focus of my faith: to Jesus Christ, the same yesterday, today and forever. Amen.

Grace Superior to Moralism

27 "It is worthy of remark, that numbers of these people are brought to a strict compliance with the rules of morality and sobriety, and to a conscientious performance of the external duties of Christianity, by the internal power and influence of divine truths—the peculiar doctrine of grace—upon their minds without their having these moral duties frequently repeated and inculcated upon them, and the contrary vices particularly exposed and spoken against. . . . Those doctrines, which had the most direct tendency to humble to the fallen creature; to show him the misery of his natural state; to bring him down to the foot of sovereign mercy, and to exalt the great Redeemer—discover the transcendent excellency and infinite preciousness, and so to recommend him to the sinner's acceptance—were the subject matter of what was delivered in public and private to them, and from time repeated and inculcated upon them.

"God was pleased to give these divine truths such a powerful influence upon the minds of these people, and so to bless them for the effectual awakening of numbers of them, that their lives were quickly reformed, without my insisting upon the precepts of morality, and spending time in repeated harangues upon external duties. There was indeed no room for any kind of discourses but those which respected the essentials of religion, and the experimental knowledge of divine things. . . . And at the same time to open to them the glorious and complete remedy provided in Christ for helpless perishing sinners, and offered freely to those who have no goodness of their own, no works of righteousness which they have done, to recommend them to God.

"This was the continued strain of my preaching; this my great concern and constant endeavour, so to enlighten the mind, as thereby duly to affect the heart, and, as far as possible, give persons a sense of feeling of these precious and important doctrines of grace, at least as far as means might conduce to it. These were the doctrines, and this the method of preaching, which were blessed of God for the awakening, and I trust, the saving conversion of number of souls." (pp. 324-25)

Prayer

All glory to you, O God; all I am I owe to you. As I progress in my spiritual trek and receive a clearer illumination of your presence, deliver me from legalistic pride. And as I seek to influence others, may it not be by means of the law but by grace. Lest I forget, may I reread the writings of Paul, Augustine, Luther, Calvin, Wesley and Brainerd, to remind me that grace —your unmerited favor and love—is all in all. Amen.

Beyond Mere Emotionalism

 "It is worthy to be noted, to the praise of sovereign grace, that amidst so great a work of conviction—so much concern and religious affection—there has been no prevalence, nor indeed any considerable appearance of false religion, if I may so term it, or heats of imagination, intemperate zeal, and spiritual pride; which corrupt mixtures too often attend the revival and powerful propagation of religion; and that there have been very few instances of irregular and scandalous behaviour among those who have appeared serious. I may justly repeat what I formerly observed, that there has here been no appearance of 'bodily agonies, convulsions, frightful screamings, swoonings,' and the like; and may now further add, that there has been no prevalence of visions, trances, and imaginations of any kind. . . .

"But this work of grace has, in the main, been carried on with a surprising degree of purity, and freedom from truth and corrupt mixture. The religious concern under which persons have been, has generally been rational and just; arising from a sense of their sins and exposedness to the divine displeasure on account of them; as well as their utter inability to deliver themselves from the misery which they felt and feared. If there has been, in any instance, an appearance of concern and perturbation of mind, when the subjects of it knew not why; yet there has been no prevalence of any such thing; and indeed I scarcely know of any instance of that nature at all. It is very remarkable, that, although the concern of many persons under convictions of their perishing state has been very great and pressing, yet I have never seen any thing like desperation attending it in any one instance. They ... have been brought to give up all hopes of deliverance from themselves; have experienced great distress and anguish of soul; and yet, in the seasons of the greatest extremity, there has been no appearance of despair in any of them—nothing that has discouraged, or in any wise hindered them from the most diligent use of all proper means for their conversion and salvation. Hence it is apparent, that there is not that danger of persons being driven into despair under spiritual trouble, unless in cases of deep and habitual melancholy, which the world in general is ready to imagine.

"The comfort which persons have obtained after their distresses, has likewise in general appeared solid, well-grounded, and scriptural; arising from a spiritual and supernatural illumination of mind—a view of divine things, in a measure, as they are, a complacency of soul in the divine perfections, and a peculiar satisfaction in the way of salvation by free sovereign grace in the great Redeemer." (pp. 330-31)

Prayer

O God of love, in the awakening of my own day I see strange phenomena. Some people profess to have had exotic experiences of your presence that I have not known. Give me discernment to differentiate between genuine emotion and mere emotionalism. In loving you, my affections have been profoundly stirred. Grant that these powerful affections may be balanced with a rational and Scriptural apprehension of your work of grace in my life, in Jesus' name. Amen.

The Worshiping Community

29 "It is remarkable, that God has so continued and renewed the showers of his grace here;—so quickly set up his visible kingdom among these people; and so smiled upon them in relation to their acquirement of knowledge, both divine and human. It is now nearly a year since the beginning of the gracious outpouring of the divine Spirit among them; and although it has often seemed to decline and abate for some short space of time—as may be observed by several passages of my Journal, where I have endeavoured to note things just as they appeared to me—yet the shower has seemed to be renewed, and the work of grace revived again. A divine influence seems still apparently to attend the means of grace, in a greater or less degree, in most of our meetings for religious exercises; whereby religious persons are refreshed, strengthened, and established, convictions revived and promoted in many instances, and some few persons newly awakened from time to time. It must be acknowledged that for some time past, there has, in general, appeared a more manifest decline of this work; and the divine Spirit has seemed, in a considerable measure, withdrawn, especially with regard to his awakening influence. . . . Yet, blessed be God, there is still an appearance of divine power and grace, a desirable degree of tenderness, religious affection and devotion in our assemblies.

"As God has continued and renewed the showers of his grace among this people for some time; so he has with uncommon quickness set up his visible kingdom, and gathered himself a church in the midst of them. I have now baptized since the conclusion of my last Journal, (or the First Part,) thirty persons, fifteen adults and fifteen children. Which added to the number there mentioned, makes seventy-seven persons; whereof thirty-eight are adults, and thirty-nine children; and all within the space of eleven months past. . . .

"I likewise administered the Lord's supper to a number of persons, who I have abundant reason to think, as I elsewhere observed, were proper subjects, of that ordinance within the space of ten months and ten days, after my first coming among these Indians in New Jersey. . . .

"There has been a wonderful thirst after Christian knowledge prevailing among them in general, and an eager desire of being instructed in Christian doctrines and manners. This has prompted them to ask many pertinent as well as important questions; the answers to which have tended much to enlighten their minds, and promote their knowledge in divine things. . . .

"They have likewise queried with me, respecting a proper method, as well as proper matter, of prayer, and expressions suitable to be used in that religious exercise; and have taken pains in order to the performance of this duty with understanding. They have likewise taken pains, and appeared remarkably apt in learning to sing Psalm-tunes, and are now able to sing with a good degree of decency in the worship of God." (pp. 327-29)

Prayer

You have called me, Eternal God, not to live my new life in isolation but within the community of the faithful, the church. How natural it seems that once my own life has been changed by your grace to seek those who participate in corporate worship. I yearn to hear your Word in Scripture, to receive the sacrament of the Lord's Supper, to pray and to sing hymns of praise. I love your kingdom, Lord. Amen.

"My Own Congregation"

30 "I know of no assembly of Christians, where there seems to
be so much of the presence of God, where brotherly love so
much prevails, and where I should take so much delight in
the public worship of God in general, as in my own congregation." (p. 282)

"Having rested sometime after the administration of the
sacrament, being extremely tired with the necessary prolix-
ity of the work, I walked from house to house, and conversed
particularly with most of the communicants, and found they
had been almost universally refreshed at the Lord's table, 'as
with new wine.' Never did I see such an appearance of Christian love among any people in all my life. It was so remarkable, that one might well have cried with an agreeable surprise, 'Behold how they love one another.' I think there could
be no greater tokens of mutual affection among the people
of God, in the early days of Christianity, than what now appeared here. The sight was so desirable, and so well becoming
the gospel, that nothing less could be said of it than that it
was 'the doing of the Lord,' the genuine operation of Him 'who
is Love.'

". . . O, what a sweet and blessed season was this! God himself, I am persuaded, was in the midst of his people, attending on his own ordinance. I doubt not but many, in the conclusion of the day, could say with their whole hearts, 'Verily,
a day thus spent in God's house, is better than a thousand

elsewhere.' The sweet union, harmony and endearing love and tenderness subsisting among them was, I thought, the most lively emblem of the heavenly world, which I had ever seen." (pp. 300-01)

"But, blessed be God! I enjoyed liberty in prayer for my dear flock, and was enabled to pour out my soul into the bosom of a tender Father. My heart within me was melted, when I came to plead for my dear people and for the kingdom of Christ in general. Oh, how sweet was this evening to my soul!" (p. 309)

Prayer

Faithful God, I desire also a congregation of people where love is shared intimately. I need the comradeship and support of such people who will encourage me in my own spiritual growth. O God, there is no greater experience than to give and receive such brotherly love within a gathered community. Praise be to you for the fellowship of saints whom I affection- ately call "my own congregation," through Jesus Christ, who binds us all together in our devotion to him and to one another. Amen.

A Social Conscience

31 "The Indians in these parts have, in times past, run themselves in debt, by their excessive drinking; and some have taken the advantage of them, and put them to trouble and charge, by arresting sundry of them; whereby it was supposed their hunting lands, in great part, were much endangered, and might speedily be taken from them. Being sensible that they could not subsist together in these parts, in order to be their being a Christian congregation, if these lands should be taken, which was thought very likely; I thought it my duty to use my utmost endeavours to prevent so unhappy an event. Having acquainted the gentlemen concerned in this mission with the affair, according to the best information I could get of it, they thought it proper to expend the money, which they had been and still were collecting for the religious interest of the Indians, at least part of it, for discharging debts, and securing these lands, that there might be no entanglement lying upon them to hinder the settlement and hopeful enlargement of a Christian congregation of Indians in these parts. Having received orders from them, I answered in behalf of the Indians, eighty-two pounds, five shillings, N. Jersey currency, at eight shillings per ounce; and so prevented the danger of difficulty in this respect.

"As God has wrought a wonderful work of grace among these Indians, and now inclines others from remote places to fall in among them almost continually; and as he has opened a door for the prevention of the difficulty now mentioned which seemed greatly to threaten their religious interests as well as worldly comforts; it is to be hoped that he designs to establish a church for himself among them, and hand down true religion to their posterity." (p. 274)

"My people were out this day with the design of clearing some of their land, above fifteen miles distant from this settlement, in order to their setting there in a compact form, where they might be under the advantages of attending the public worship of God, of having their children taught in a school, and at the same time have a conveniency for planting: their land, in the place of our present residence, being of little or no value for that purpose. . . . I endeavoured to press the importance of their being laborious, diligent, and vigorous in the prosecution of their business; especially at the present juncture, the season of planting being now near, in order to their being in a capacity of living together, and enjoying the means of grace and instruction." (pp. 290-91)

Prayer

God of Justice, what really happened at the massacre in Wounded Knee in 1890? What really happened at the confrontation in Wounded Knee in 1973? In my comfortable existence, the recollection of such incidents receives only scant attention. And yet, the more I reflect upon our national treatment of the Indians—broken treaties, personal indignities and the plunder of their lands—the more I realize that apathy like my own has contributed to such shame. Raise up in our generation, O God, advocates who will plead the cause of the Indians and of all the dispossessed peoples of the world. Begin with the arousal of my own social conscience. Amen.

Indians and Whites Commune Together

"Being desired by the Rev. William Tennent to be his assistant in the administration of the Lord's Supper, I this morning rode to Freehold to render that assistance. My people also being invited to attend the sacramental solemnity; they cheerfully embraced the opportunity, and this day attended the preparatory services with me. . . .

"Most of my people, who had been communicants at the Lord's table, before being present at this sacramental occasion, communed with others in the holy ordinance, at the desire, and I trust to the satisfaction and comfort of numbers of God's people, who had longed to see this day, and whose hearts had rejoiced in this work of grace among the Indians, which prepared the way for what appeared so agreeable at this time. Those of my people who communed, seemed in general, agreeable affected at the Lord's table, and some of them considerably melted with the love of Christ, although they were not so remarkably refreshed and feasted at this time, as when I administer this ordinance to them in our own congregation only. A number of my dear people sat down by themselves at the last table; at which time God seemed to be in the midst of them. Some of the by-standers were affected with seeing those who had been 'aliens from the common wealth of Israel, and strangers to the covenant of promise,' who of all men had lived 'without hope and without God in the world,' now brought near to God, as his professing people, and sealing their covenant with him, by a solemn and devout attendance upon this sacred ordinance. As numbers of God's people were refreshed with this sight, and thereby excited to bless God for the enlargement of his kingdom in the world; so some others, I was told, were awakened by it, apprehending the danger they were in of being themselves finally cast out; while they saw others from the east and west preparing, and hopefully prepared in some good measure, to sit down in the kingdom of God. . . .

"In the evening I could not but rejoice in God, and bless him in the manifestations of grace in the day past. Oh it was a sweet and solemn day and evening! a season of comfort to the godly, and of awakening to some souls! O that I could praise the Lord. . . .

"After my people had attended the concluding exercises of the sacramental solemnity, they returned home; many of them rejoicing for all the goodness of God which they had seen and felt." (pp. 316-18)

Prayer

O God, may the poignant simplicity of this communion service be a paradigm to me of what the church is meant to be. I pray that the church will increasingly represent the rich diversity of red, black, brown, yellow and white people in the world. And just as in Brainerd's day such a unique expression of Christian unity prompted certain observers to seek Christ, so may the oneness of our own fellowship today persuade others to believe in the same Christ who is our Lord too. Amen.

UNION
WITH GOD

Northampton, Massachusetts.
Jonathan Edwards' house, where Brainerd spent
the last months of his life.

"I see the value of Christian biography tonight, as I have been reading Brainerd's Diary.... Enjoyed much sweetness (as he puts it) in the reading of the last months of Brainerd's life.... was much encouraged to think of a life of godliness in the light of an early death."[1]

Jim Elliot,
martyred missionary to the
Auca Indians, 1956

"But is the human soul, or self, ever actually merged with God in such a manner as to lose its own identity, even for a transient moment?"[2] David Brainerd would have undoubtedly answered such a question in the negative. Although he testified to the most intimate kind of communion with God and used such graphic, mystical references as "my own nothingness" and "I was swallowed up in God," he did not believe that actual union with God was possible in his own lifetime. There was no annihilation of human personality or absorption into the divine. Man was still man, and God was still God. But now, with death imminent, Brainerd yearned passionately for a new dimension of his relationship with God;

now he wished not just to glorify God, but "to behold his glory."

The historical summary of his last year begins in the fall of 1746. Despite his amazing success among the Indians at Crossweeksung and Cranberry, the entries in his diary indicate that he would have to curtail his missionary activities. "Coughing blood" more often now, he decided to head northward where he stopped to visit old friends, such as Jonathan Dickinson in Elizabethtown and Aaron Burr in Newark. Eventually he received an invitation to stay at the home of Jonathan Edwards in Northampton, Massachusetts. Except for a brief visit to Boston, the remaining months of Brainerd's life were spent in Northampton.

Although desperately ill, Brainerd was not idle during his stay in Edwards' home. He continued to keep his diary, prayed, studied the Scriptures and wrote a variety of letters. He even wrote a preface to Thomas Shepard's *Meditations and Spiritual Experiences* which was published in 1747. Shepard, a former pastor of the Cambridge Church (1636-1649) was recommended by Brainerd to young converts of the Great Awakening as an excellent Puritan guide for interpreting Christian experience and for maintaining a creative balance between reason and the affections. And, of course, Brainerd highly recommended Edwards' own *Treatise on Religious Affections* as a penetrating analysis of true and false affections. Such an exploration of motives as found in both Shepard and Edwards would lead one away from self-love, Brainerd was convinced, and toward what was later to be called "disinterested benevolence" in the service of God and men.

A moving personal sidelight involving Brainerd and Jerusha, one of Edwards' daughters, should be mentioned. Brainerd had corresponded earlier with Jerusha, and in time their love for one another became more intimate. After Brainerd was no longer able to continue his diary, Edwards records in his notes part of a conversation between the young couple.

Said David to Jerusha: "If I thought I should not see you, and be happy with you in another world, I could not bear to part with you. But we shall spend an happy eternity together."[3]

Completely "burned out" in the service of God, David Brainerd died at Northampton on October 9, 1747, at the age of twenty-nine. Jerusha, who attended the dying young man during his last year, contracted the same disease of tuberculosis and died a few months later at the tender age of eighteen.

The following eight selections include some of Brainerd's later devotional impressions. Meditating upon these thoughts should help us in interpreting the meaning of the last stage of our own spiritual trek, namely, union with God. The first three selections, focusing upon his decision to conclude his mission venture to the Indians and return to New England, provide us with useful insights in facing our own adjustments to sudden illness, retirement and death itself. The next three selections consist of excerpts from three letters Brainerd wrote (to use his own words: "on the verge of eternity") to his brother Israel (a student at Yale College), to an anonymous ministerial student and to his brother John, who had succeeded him as a missionary to the Indians. These three excerpts stressing experiential faith, continual self-discipline and the necessity of distinguishing between true and false religion are still wise counsel for those who seek a balanced Christian view of mysticism and mission in the midst of the present quest for transcendence. The first of the final two selections reminds us of the practical value of keeping a personal diary or journal to record our inner reflections in the presence of God. And the last selection points us toward the goal of our spiritual journey and our ultimate happiness —to behold God's glory in eternity.

The Journey Falters

33 "I was so weak that I could not preach, nor pretend to ride over to my people in the forenoon. In the afternoon, rode out; sat in my chair, and discoursed to my people from Rom. xiv. 7, 8 'For none of us liveth to himself,' &c. I was strengthened and helped in my discourse; and there appeared something agreeable in the assembly. I returned to my lodgings extremely tired, but thankful, that I had been enabled to speak a word to my poor people, from whom I had been so long absent. Was enabled to sleep very little this night, through weariness and pain. O how blessed should I be, if the little I do were all done with right views! Oh that, 'whether I live, I might live to the Lord; or whether I die, I might die unto the Lord; that, whether living or dying, I might be the Lord's!'

"Spent this day, as well as the whole week past, under a great degree of bodily weakness, exercised with a violent cough, and a considerable fever. I had no appetite for any kind of food; and frequently brought up what I ate, as soon as it was down; oftentimes had little rest in my bed, owing to pains in my breast and back. I was able, however, to ride over to my people, about two miles, every day, and take some care of those who were then at work upon a small house for me to reside in among the Indians. I was sometimes scarce able to walk, and never able to sit up the whole day, through the week. Was calm and composed, and but little exercised with melancholy, as in former seasons of weakness. Whether I should ever recover or no, seemed very doubtful; but this was many times a comfort to me, that life and death did not depend upon my choice. I was pleased to think, that He who is infinitely wise, had the determination of this matter; and that I had no trouble to consider and weigh things upon all sides, in order to make the choice, whether I should live or die. Thus my time was consumed; I had little strength to pray, none to write or read, and scarce any to meditate; but through divine goodness, I could with great composure look death in the face, and frequently with sensible joy. O how blessed it is, to be habitually prepared for death! The Lord grant, that I may be actually ready also!" (pp. 383-84)

"Was composed and comfortable, willing either to die or live; but found it hard to be reconciled to the thoughts of living useless. Oh that I might never live to be a burden to God's creation; but that I might be allowed to repair home, when my sojourning work is done." (p. 387)

Prayer

Lord of all seasons, prepare me for that juncture in my spiritual pilgrimage when I will have to revise my own mission venture. Create in me a flexible mind so that I will be able to make the necessary adjustments to unexpected illness or a drastically reduced schedule. Help me to find my way along this new path and lead me toward the ultimate destination which you have charted for me. Into your faithful keeping I commit this one day and all the remaining days of my life, in the name of Christ my Lord. Amen.

A Time of Parting

"Being now in so weak and low a state, that I was utterly incapable of performing my work, and having little hope of recovery, unless by much riding, I thought it my duty to take a long journey into New-England, and to divert myself among my friends, whom I had not seen for a long time. Accordingly I took leave of my congregation this day. —Before I left my people, I visited them all in their respective houses, and discoursed to each one, as I thought most proper and suitable for their circumstances, and found great freedom and assistance in so doing. I scarcely left one house but some were in tears; and many were not only affected with my being about to leave them, but with the solemn addresses I made them upon divine things; for I was helped to be fervent in spirit, while I discoursed to them. When I had thus gone through my congregation, which took me most of the day, and had taken leave of them, and of the school, I left home, and rode about two miles to the house where I lived in the summer past and there lodged. Was refreshed, this evening, because I had left my congregation so well-disposed and affected, and had been so much assisted in making my farewell addresses to them." (p. 389)

"After this, having perhaps taken some cold, I began to decline as to bodily health; and continued to do so, till the latter end of January 1747. Having a violent cough, a considerable fever, an asthmatic disorder, and no appetite for any manner of food, nor any power of digestion. I was reduced to so low a state, that my friends, I believe, generally despaired of my life; and some of them, for some time together, thought I could scarce live a day. At this time, I could think of nothing, with any application of mind, and seemed to be in a great measure void of all affection, and was exercised with great temptations; but yet was not, ordinarily, afraid of death." (p. 391)

"On Friday morning, I rose early, walked about among my people, and enquired into their state and concerns. . . . About ten o'clock, I called my people together, and after having explained and sung a psalm, I prayed with them. There was a considerable deal of affection among them; I doubt not, in some instances, that which was more than merely natural." (p. 393)

Prayer

God of comfort, you have provided many friends to accompany me and encourage me along my way. How difficult it is to part from close and dear friends. I am grateful for these companions, especially for those who have been coworkers in the service of Christ. Grant me both the courage to accept the severance of these ties of camaraderie and the determination to center my thoughts supremely on you whose faithfulness and loving kindness are forever and ever. Amen.

Traveling Homeward

35 "This day [April 20, 1747] I arrived at the age of twenty-nine years.

"I set out on my journey for New-England, in order (if it might be the will of God) to recover my health by riding." (p. 396)

"Towards noon, I saw, that the grace of God in Christ, is infinitely free towards sinners, and such sinners as I was. I also saw, that God is the supreme good, that in his presence is life; and I began to long to die, that I might be with him, in a state of freedom from all sin. O how a small glimpse of his excellency refreshed my soul! O how worthy is the blessed God to be loved, adored, and delighted in, for himself, for his own divine excellencies!

"Though I felt much dullness, and want of a spirit of prayer, this week; yet I had some glimpses of the excellency of divine things; and especially one morning, in secret meditation and prayer, the excellency and beauty of holiness, as a likeness to the glorious God, was so discovered to me, that I began to long earnestly to be in that world where holiness dwells in perfection. I seemed to long for this perfect holiness, not so much for the sake of my own happiness, although I saw clearly that this was the greatest, yea, the only happiness of the soul, as that I might please God, live entirely to him, and glorify him to the utmost stretch of my rational powers and capacities." (pp. 397-98)

"[At Northampton] my attention was greatly engaged, and my soul so drawn forth, this day, by what I heard of the 'exceeding preciousness of the saving grace of God's Spirit,' that it almost overcame my body in my weak state. I saw that true grace is exceedingly precious indeed; that it is very rare; and that there is but a very small degree of it, even where the reality of it is to be found; At least I saw this to be my case.

"In the preceding week, I enjoyed some comfortable seasons of meditation. One morning, the cause of God appeared exceedingly precious to me. The Redeemer's kingdom is all that is valuable in the earth, and I could not but long for the promotion of it in the world. I saw also, that this cause is God's, that he has an infinitely greater regard and concern for it, than I could possibly have; that if I have any true love to this blessed interest it is only a drop derived from that ocean. Hence I was ready to 'lift up my head with joy;' and conclude, 'Well, if God's cause be so dear and precious to him, he will promote it.' Thus I did as it were, rest on God that he would surely promote that which was so agreeable to his own will; though the time when, must still be left to his sovereign pleasure." (p. 400)

Prayer

O Lord, the time arrives when the prospect of death becomes real and such knowledge shakes even the most faithful of us. I realize that people all around me die, but how different it is when I acknowledge that fact that I too will die. But how assuring it is to know that I belong to a community with a destiny and that that to which I have committed myself will transcend even death itself. O Lord, even when I am no longer able to continue my mission with full vigor, may I not dismay about its eventual outcome because it is "your cause" and you will surely see that it prospers according to your sovereign will, for the sake of Jesus. Amen.

"On the Verge of Eternity"

36 "It is on the verge of Eternity I now address you. I am heartily sorry, that I have so little strength to write what I long so much to communicate to you. But let me tell you, my brother, Eternity is another thing than we ordinarily take it to be in a healthful state. O, how vast and boundless! O how fixed and unalterable! O, of what infinite importance is it, that we be prepared for Eternity! I have been just a dying, now for more than a week; and all around me have thought me so. I have had clear views of Eternity; have seen the blessedness of the godly, in some measure; and have longed to share their happy state; as well as been comfortably satisfied, that through grace, I shall do so. . . . O, my brother, let me then beseech you now to examine, whether you are indeed a new creature? whether you have ever acted above self? whether the glory of God has ever been the sweetest and highest concern with you? whether you have ever been reconciled to all the perfections of God? in a word, whether God has been your portion, and a holy conformity to him your chief delight? If you cannot answer positively, consider seriously the frequent breathings of your soul; but do not however put yourself off with a slight answer. If you have reason to think you are graceless, O give yourself and the throne of grace no rest, till God arise and save. But if the case should be otherwise, bless God for his grace, and press after holiness.

"My soul longs, that you should be fitted for, and in due

time go into the work of the ministry. I cannot bear to think of your going into any other business in life. Do not be discouraged, because you see your elder brothers in the ministry die early, one after another. I declare now I am dying, I would not have spent my life otherwise for the whole world. But I must leave this with God." (pp. 404-05)

Prayer

Everlasting Father, enable me to live "on the verge of Eternity." Grant me the long perspective of the future from which to evaluate the past and the present. Help me to see things as they really are and not as I sometimes mistakenly believe they are. Assure me that even when I do not perceive you present at any given moment yet I may have confidence that you are the God who leads me into tomorrow. And to those who are newly awakened by your Spirit in our own day, I pray that you will grant them the perspective of eternity not just in their dying moments but all the days of their life. Grant this prayer through Jesus Christ who has brought us eternal life, which is both a present reality and a future hope. Amen.

"Live to God"

"How amazing it is, that the living who know they must die, should notwithstanding, 'put far away the evil,' in a season of health and prosperity; and live at such an awful distance from a familiarity with the grave and the great concern beyond it! . . . How rare are the instances of those who live and act, from day to day; as on the verge of Eternity; striving to fill up all their remaining moments in the service, and to the honour of their great Master! We insensibly trifle away time, while we seem to have enough of it; and are so strangely amused, as in a great measure to lose a sense of the holiness and blessed qualifications necessary to prepare us to be inhabitants of the heavenly paradise. But O, dear Sir, a dying bed, if we enjoy our reason clearly, will give another view of things. I have now, for more than three weeks, lain under the greatest degree of weakness; the greater part of the time, expecting daily and hourly to enter into the eternal world: sometimes have been so far gone, as to be wholly speechless, for some hours together. O of what vast importance has a holy spiritual life appeared to me at this season! I have longed to call upon all my friends, to make it their business to live to God; and especially all that are designed for, or engaged in the service of the sanctuary. O dear Sir, do not think it enough, to live at the rate of common Christians. Alas, to how little purpose do they often converse, when they meet together! The visits, even of those who are called Christians indeed, are frequently extremely barren; and conscience cannot but condemn us for the misimprovement of time, while we have been conversant with them. But the way to enjoy the divine presence, and to be fitted for distinguishing service for God, is to live a life of great devotion and constant self-dedication to him; observing the motions and dispositions of our own hearts, whence we may learn the corruptions that lodge there, and our constant need of help from God for the performance of the least duty. And O dear Sir, let me beseech you frequently to attend the great and precious duties of secret fasting and prayer.

"I have a secret thought, from some things I have observed, that God may perhaps design you for some singular service in the world. . . . Suffer me therefore, finally, to intreat you earnestly to give yourself to prayer, to reading and meditation on divine truths: strive to penetrate to the bottom of them, and never be content with a superficial knowledge. By this means, your thoughts will gradually grow weighty and judicious; and you hereby will be possessed of a valuable treasure, out of which you may produce 'things new and old,' to the glory of God." (pp. 405-06)

Prayer

Eternal God, I praise you for the gift of time. May I use it wisely in cultivating my inner life of prayer, Scripture reading and contemplation so that I may be more freely disposed to be your effective servant. Raise up in our generation young men and women with a sense of urgency to do your will. May they too realize that God may indeed have "some singular service in the world" for them to discharge. I pray in the name of the One who personified in his life the creative potential of the wholly committed life. Amen.

Distinguishing True and False Religion

38 "And now, my dear brother . . . labour to distinguish between true and false religion; and to that end, watch the motions of God's spirit upon your own heart. Look to him for help; and impartially compare your experiences with his word. Read Mr. Edwards on the affections; where the essence and soul of religion is clearly distinguished from false affections. Value religious joys according to the subject-matter of them: there are many who rejoice in their supposed justification; but what do these joys argue, but only they love themselves? Whereas, in true spiritual joys, the soul rejoices in God for what he is in himself; blesses God for his holiness, sovereignty, power, faithfulness, and all his perfections; adores God, that he is what he is, that he is unchangeably possessed of infinite glory and happiness. Now, when men thus rejoice in the perfections of God, and in the infinite excellency of the way of salvation by Christ, and in the holy commands of God, which are a transcript of his holy nature; these joys are divine and spiritual. Our joys will stand by us at the hour of death, if we can be then satisfied, that we have thus acted above self; and in a disinterested manner, if I may so express it, rejoiced in the glory of the blessed God. I fear, you are not sufficiently aware how much false religion there is in the world; many serious Christians and valuable ministers are too easily imposed upon this false blaze. I likewise fear, you are not sensible of the dreadful effects and consequences of this false religion. Let me tell you, it is 'the devil transformed into an angel of light;' it is a fiend of hell, that always springs up with every revival of religion, and stabs and murders the cause of God, while it passes current with multitudes of well meaning people for the height of religion. Set yourself, my brother, to crush all appearances of this nature, among the Indians, and never encourage any degrees of heat without light. Charge my people in the name of their dying minister, yes in the name of 'Him who was dead and is alive,' to live and walk as becomes the gospel. . . .

"God knows, I was heartily willing to have served him longer in the work of the ministry, although it had still been attended with all the labours and hardships of past years, if he had seen fit that it should be so: but as his will now appears otherwise, I am fully content, and can with the utmost freedom say, 'The will of the Lord be done.' " (pp. 407-09)

Prayer

O God of light and wisdom, in the midst of current religious and pseudo-religious enthusiasm enable me to distinguish between the real and the counterfeit. May I not absolutize my own spiritual adventure nor ostracize all who do not fit into the same pattern. Help me to compare my own inner experience with the Scriptures. Does my personal faith impel me to move out in benevolent social action on behalf of those who suffer from demeaning poverty, racial discrimination, the arrogance of political power and the ravages of war? Is my aim to live for self or for your glory? Grant me discernment, O God, as I meditate upon the life of Jesus, my supreme example, my Savior and my Lord, in whose name I pray. Amen.

The Journey in Retrospect

39 "I began to read some of my private writings, which my brother brought me; and was considerably refreshed with what I found in them.

"I proceeded further in reading my old private writings, and found that they had the same effect upon me as before. I could not but rejoice and bless God for what passed long ago, which without writing had been entirely lost." (p. 418)

"I thought of dignity in heaven; but instantly the thought returned, 'I do not go to heaven to get honour, but to give all possible glory and praise.' O how I longed that God should be glorified on earth also! O I was made—for eternity,—if God might be glorified! Bodily pains I cared not for; though I was then in extremity, I never felt easier. I felt willing to glorify God in that state of bodily distress, as long as he pleased I should continue in it. The grave appeared really sweet, and I longed to lodge my weary bones in it: but Oh, that God might be glorified! this was the burden of all my cry. . . . O to love and praise God more, to please him forever! This my soul panted after, and even now pants for while I write. Oh that God might be glorified in the whole earth! 'Lord let thy kingdom come.' I longed for a spirit of preaching to descend and rest on ministers, that they might address the consciences of men with closeness and power. I saw that God 'had the residue of the Spirit;' and my soul longed that it should be 'poured from on high.' I could not but plead with God for my dear congregation, that he would preserve it, and not suffer his great name to lose its glory in that work; my soul still longing, that God might be glorified." (p. 421)

Prayer

O God of the ages, teach me to preserve in writing my private meditations. May I record my spiritual thoughts so that they may be a source of comfort and clarification to me in later years when I trace the windings of your grace throughout the course of my pilgrimage. I am grateful especially for the long enduring chain of influence Brainerd's diary has had in inspiring so many people to explore the inner life and engage in active mission throughout the world since his day to the present. Bless all those who communicate and perpetuate the Christian good news and encourage more and more dedicated people to develop a ministry of writing whether it be a letter to a friend in need or a grand apology for the faith. Hear my prayers, in the name of the One who was the Word made flesh, even Christ Jesus my Lord. Amen.

"To Behold His Glory"

"I endeavoured again to do something by way of writing, but soon found my powers of body and mind utterly fail. Felt not so sweetly, as when I was able to do something which I hoped would do some good. In the evening was discomposed and wholly delirious; but it was not long before God was pleased to give me some sleep, and fully composed my mind. O blessed be God for his great goodness to me.... He has, except those few minutes, given me the clear exercise of my reason, and enabled me to labour much for him, in things both of a public and private nature; and perhaps to do more good, than I should have done if I had been well; besides the comfortable influences of his blessed Spirit, with which he has been pleased to refresh my soul. May his name have all the glory for ever and ever. Amen.

"My soul was this day, at turns, sweetly set on God: I longed to be with him, that I might behold his glory. I felt sweetly disposed to commit all to him, even my dearest friends, my dearest flock, my absent brother, and all my concerns for time and eternity. O that his kingdom might come in the world; that they might all love and glorify him, for what he is in himself; and that the blessed Redeemer might see of the travail of his soul and be satisfied! 'O, come, Lord Jesus, come quickly! Amen.' " (pp. 428-29) [These are the last words that Brainerd recorded in his diary.]

Prayer

O God of the Beginning and of the End, I move eventually to the Omega point of my journey. Throughout my walk with you I have sought to glorify you and you have given me gracious signs of your presence along the way, even in my darkest moments. And now in David Brainerd's words, I aspire "to behold your glory." You were the One who loved me before I ever thought of loving you. You called me to begin this journey of faith, and now I return to the origin of my new life. Help me to believe that this is not the end but the climax of my adventure —the time when I shall see you face to face in the luminous brightness of your glory, through Jesus Christ my Lord. Amen.

Notes

Introduction

[1]Ronald M. Enroth, Edward E. Ericson, Jr., and C. Breckinridge Peters, *The Jesus People: Old-Time Religion in the Age of Aquarius* (Grand Rapids: Eerdmans, 1972), p. 223.

[2]Sereno E. Dwight, ed., *Memoirs of the Rev. David Brainerd: Missionary to the Indians . . . Chiefly Taken from His Own Diary by Rev. Jonathan Edwards . . .* (New Haven: printed and published by S. Converse, 1822), p. 34.

Part I

[1]Kenneth Scott Latourette, *A History of the Expansion of Christianity* (New York: Harper & Brothers, 1939), III, 220.

[2]Dag Hammarskjold, *Markings* (New York: Alfred A. Knopf, 1965), p. 205.

[3]Mark Hatfield, *Conflict and Conscience* (Waco, Tex.: Word Books, 1971), p. 98.

[4]*Memoirs,* p. 52.

Part II

[1]Constance E. Padwick, *Henry Martyn, Confessor of the Faith* (London: Student Christian Movement, 1922), p. 89.

[2]Georgia Harkness, *Mysticism: Its Meaning and Message* (Nashville: Abingdon Press, 1973), p. 22.

[3]Robert S. Paul, *The Atonement and the Sacraments* (Nashville: Abingdon Press, 1960), p. 131.

Part III

[1]*Memoirs,* pp. 31-32.

[2]John of the Cross, "O Happy Night," quoted in George A. Barrois, ed., *Pathways of the Inner Life* (Indianapolis: Bobbs-Merrill, 1956), p. 146.

[3]Frank Laubach, *Channels of Spiritual Power* (Old Tappan, N.J.: Fleming H. Revell, 1954), p. 23.

[4]*Memoirs,* pp. 439-40.

[5]David Wynbeek, *David Brainerd, Beloved Yankee* (Grand Rapids: Eerdmans, 1961), p. 142.

Part IV

[1]John Wesley, *Works* (Grand Rapids: Zondervan, 1958), VIII, 328. Reproduced from the authorized edition published by the Wesleyan Conference Office in London, England, in 1872.

[2]Evelyn Underhill, *Mysticism* (London: Methuen & Co., 1948), p. 169.

[3]Sheldon Smith, Robert Handy and Lefferts Loetscher, *American Christianity* (New York: Charles Scribner's Sons, 1960), I, 314-15.

[4]*Memoirs,* p. 313.

[5]*Memoirs,* pp. 319-20.

Part V

[1]Elisabeth Elliot, *Shadow of the Almighty: The Life and Testament of Jim Elliot* (New York: Harper & Brothers, 1958), p. 108.

[2]Harkness, *Mysticism: Its Meaning and Message,* p. 23.

[3]*Memoirs,* p. 429.